LEVELS OF LIFE

JULIAN BARNES

LEVELS OF LIFE

JONATHAN CAPE

LONDON

Published by Jonathan Cape 2013

2 4 6 8 10 9 7 5 3 1

First published in Great Britain in 2013 by Jonathan Cape
Random House, 20 Vauxhall Bridge Road,
London SW1V 2SA
www.randomhouse.co.uk

Addresses for companies within The Random House Group Limited
can be found at: www.randomhouse.co.uk/offices.htm
The Random House Group Limited Reg. No. 954009

A CIP catalogue record for this book is available
from the British Library
ISBN 9780224098151

The Random House Group Limited makes every effort to
ensure that the papers used in its books are made from trees that have
been legally sourced from well-managed and credibly certified forests.
Our paper procurement policy can be found at:
www.randomhouse.co.uk/paper.htm

Printed and bound in Great Britain by
Clays Ltd, St Ives PLC

for Pat

CONTENTS

THE SIN OF HEIGHT

ON THE LEVEL

THE LOSS OF DEPTH

THE SIN OF HEIGHT

You put together two things that have not been put together before. And the world is changed. People may not notice at the time, but that doesn't matter. The world has been changed nonetheless.

Colonel Fred Burnaby of the Royal Horse Guards, member of the Council of the Aeronautical Society, took off from the Dover Gasworks on the 23rd of March 1882, and landed halfway between Dieppe and Neufchâtel.

Sarah Bernhardt had taken off from the centre of Paris four years previously, and landed near Emerainville in the *département* of Seine-et-Marne.

Félix Tournachon had taken off from the Champ de Mars in Paris on the 18th of October 1863; after being driven east by a gale for seventeen hours, he crash-landed close to a railway line near Hanover.

Fred Burnaby travelled alone, in a red-and-yellow balloon called *The Eclipse*. Its basket was five feet long, three feet wide and three feet high. Burnaby weighed seventeen stone, wore a striped coat and a close skullcap, and to protect his neck from the sun made a puggaree of his handkerchief. He took with him two beef sandwiches, a bottle of Apollinaris mineral water, a barometer to measure altitude, a thermometer, compass, and a supply of cigars.

Sarah Bernhardt travelled with her artist–lover Georges Clairin and a professional aeronaut in an orange balloon called *Doña Sol*, after her current role at the Comédie-Française. At six thirty in the evening, an hour into their flight, the actress played mother, preparing *tartines de foie gras*. The aeronaut opened a bottle of champagne, firing the cork into the sky; Bernhardt drank from a silver goblet. Then they ate oranges and tossed the empty bottle into the Lake of Vincennes. In their sudden superiority, they cheerfully dropped ballast on to the groundlings below: a family of English tourists on the balcony of the Bastille Column; later, a wedding party enjoying a rural picnic.

Tournachon travelled with eight companions in an aerostat of his own boastful imagining: 'I shall make a balloon – the Ultimate Balloon – of extraordinarily gigantic proportions, twenty times bigger than the biggest.' He called it *The Giant*. It made five flights between 1863 and 1867. Passengers on this second flight included Tournachon's wife Ernestine, the aeronaut brothers Louis and Jules Godard, and a descendant of the primal ballooning family of Montgolfier. It is not reported what food they took with them.

These were the balloon-going classes of the day: the enthusiastic English amateur, happy to be mocked as a 'balloonatic', and prepared to climb into anything about to become airborne; the most famous actress of her era, making a celebrity flight; and the professional balloonist who launched *The Giant* as a commercial venture. Two hundred thousand spectators watched its first ascent, for which thirteen passengers each paid one thousand francs; the aerostat's cradle, which resembled a two-storey wicker cottage, contained a refreshment room, beds, a lavatory, a photographic department, and even a printing room to produce instant commemorative brochures.

The Godard brothers were everywhere. They designed and built *The Giant*, and after its first two flights brought it to London for exhibition at the Crystal Palace. Shortly afterwards a third brother, Eugène Godard, brought over an even bigger fire balloon, which made two ascents from Cremorne Gardens. Its cubic capacity was twice that of *The Giant*, while its straw-fed furnace, together with chimney, weighed 980 lb. On its first London flight, Eugène agreed to take one English passenger with him, at a charge of five pounds. That man was Fred Burnaby.

These balloonists happily conformed to national stereotype. Becalmed above the English Channel, Burnaby, 'careless of the escaping gases', lights a cigar to help him think. When two French fishing boats signal for him to descend and be picked up from the water, he responds 'by dropping a copy of *The Times* for their edification' – hinting, presumably, that a practical English officer can manage perfectly well by himself, thank you, Mossoo. Sarah Bernhardt confesses that she is temperamentally drawn to ballooning because 'my dreamy nature would constantly transport me to the higher regions'. On her short flight she is provided with the convenience of a plain, straw-seated chair. When publishing her account of the adventure, Bernhardt whimsically opts to tell it from the chair's point of view.

The aeronaut would descend from the heavens, look for a flat landing place, pull on the valve-line, throw out the grapnel, and often bounce forty or fifty feet back into the air before the flukes of the anchor took hold. Then the local population would come running. When Fred Burnaby landed near the Château de Montigny, an inquisitive rustic poked his head into the half-deflated gasbag, and nearly suffocated. The locals willingly helped collapse and fold the balloon; and Burnaby found these poor French labourers much kinder and more courteous than their English equivalents. He disbursed a half-sovereign in their direction, pedantically specifying the exchange rate at the time he had left Dover. A hospitable farmer, M Barthélemy Delanray, offered to put the aeronaut up for the night. First, though, came Mme Delanray's dinner: *omelette aux oignons*, sautéed pigeon with chestnuts, vegetables, Neufchâtel cheese, cider, a bottle of Bordeaux and coffee. Afterwards, the village doctor arrived, and the butcher with a bottle of champagne. Burnaby lit a fireside cigar and reflected that 'a balloon descent in Normandy was certainly preferable to one in Essex'.

Near Emerainville, the peasants who chased after the descending balloon marvelled to see that it contained a woman. Bernhardt was used to making entrances: did she ever make a grander one than this? She was, of course, recognised. The rustics duly entertained her with a drama of their own: the tale of a grisly murder recently committed just there, exactly where she sat (on her listening and narrating chair). Soon, it came on to rain; the actress, famous for her slimness, joked that she was too thin to get wet – she would simply slip between the drops. Then, after the ritual distribution of tips, the balloon and its crew were escorted to Emerainville station in time for the last train back to Paris.

They knew it was dangerous. Fred Burnaby nearly collided with the gasworks chimney shortly after take-off. The *Doña Sol* nearly came down in a wood shortly before landing. When *The Giant* crashed close to the railway line, the experienced Godards prudently jumped out before the final impact; Tournachon broke a leg, and his wife suffered injuries to her neck and chest. A gas balloon might explode; a fire balloon, unsurprisingly, could catch fire. Every take-off and landing was hazardous. Nor did larger mean safer: it meant – as the case of *The Giant* proved – more at the mercy of the wind. Early cross-Channel aeronauts often wore cork buoyancy jackets in case they landed on water. And there were no parachutes. In August 1786 – ballooning's infancy – a young man had dropped to his death in Newcastle from a height of several hundred feet. He was one of those who held the balloon's restraining ropes; when a gust of wind suddenly shifted the airbag, his companions let go, while he held on and was borne upwards. Then he fell back to earth. As one modern historian puts it: 'The impact drove his legs into a flower bed as far as his knees, and ruptured his internal organs, which burst out on to the ground.'

Aeronauts were the new Argonauts, their adventures instantly chronicled. A balloon flight linked town and country, England and France, France and Germany. Landing provoked pure excitement: a balloon brought no evil. By the Normandy fireside of M Barthélemy Delanray, the village doctor proposed a toast to universal brotherhood. Burnaby and his new friends clinked glasses. At which point, being British, he explained to them the superiority of a monarchy over a republic. But then, the president of the Aeronautical Society of Great Britain was His Grace the Duke of Argyll, and its three vice presidents were His Grace the Duke of Sutherland, the Rt Hon. the Earl of Dufferin, and the Rt Hon. Lord Richard Grosvenor MP. The equivalent French body, the Société des Aéronautes, founded by Tournachon, was more democratic and intellectual. Its aristocrats were writers and artists: George Sand, Dumas *père et fils*, Offenbach.

Ballooning represented freedom — yet a freedom subservient to the powers of wind and weather. Aeronauts often couldn't tell if they were moving or stationary, gaining height or losing it. In the early days, they would throw out a handful of feathers, which would fly upwards if they were descending, and down if ascending. By Burnaby's time this technology had advanced to torn-up strips of newspaper. As for measuring horizontal progress, Burnaby invented his own speedometer, consisting of a small paper parachute attached to fifty yards of silk line. He would toss the parachute overboard and time how long it took for the line to run out. Seven seconds translated into a balloon speed of twelve miles per hour.

There were multiple attempts, over that first century of flight, to master this uncontrollable bag with its dangling basket. Rudders and oars were tried, pedals and wheels turning screw-fans; they all made slight difference. Burnaby believed that shape was the key: an aerostat in the form of a tube or cigar, and propelled by machinery, was the way forward – as it eventually proved. But all, whether English or French, conservative or progressive, agreed that the future of flight lay in the heavier-than-air machine. And though his name was always linked to ballooning, Tournachon also founded the Society for the Encouragement of Aerial Locomotion by Means of Heavier-than-Air Machines; its first secretary was Jules Verne. Another enthusiast, Victor Hugo, said that a balloon was like a beautiful, drifting cloud – whereas what humanity needed was the equivalent of that gravity-defying miracle, the bird. Flight, in France, was generally a matter for social progressives. Tournachon wrote that the three supreme emblems of modernity were 'photography, electricity and aeronautics'.

In the beginning, birds flew, and God made the birds. Angels flew, and God made the angels. Men and women had long legs and empty backs, and God had made them like that for a reason. To mess with flight was to mess with God. It was to prove a long struggle, full of instructive legends.

For instance, the case of Simon Magus. The National Gallery in London owns an altarpiece by Benozzo Gozzoli; its predella has been broken up and dispersed over the centuries. One section illustrates the story of St Peter, Simon Magus and the Emperor Nero. Simon was a magician who had won Nero's favour, and sought to keep it by proving that his powers were greater than those of the apostles Peter and Paul. This tiny painting tells the story in three parts. In the background is a wooden tower, from which Simon Magus is demonstrating his latest trick: human flight. Vertical take-off and lift have been achieved, and the Roman aeronaut is seen heading skywards, with only the bottom half of his green mantle showing; the rest is cut off by the picture's top edge. Simon's secret rocket fuel is, however, illegitimate: he relies – physically as well as spiritually – on the support of demons. In the mid-ground, St Peter is shown praying to God, asking Him to dispossess the demons of their power. The theological and aeronautical results of this intervention are confirmed in the foreground: a dead magician, blood oozing from his mouth after an enforced crash-landing. The sin of height is punished.

Icarus messed with the Sun God: that was a bad idea too.

The first ever ascent in a hydrogen balloon was made by the physicist Dr J. A. C. Charles on the 1st of December 1783. 'When I felt myself escaping from the earth,' he commented, 'my reaction was not pleasure but *happiness*.' It was 'a moral feeling', he added. 'I could *hear myself living*, so to speak.' Most aeronauts felt something like that, even Fred Burnaby, who made a point of not rising easily to rapture. High above the English Channel, he observes the steam from the Dover and Calais packet boat, reflects on the latest foolish and abominable plan to build a Channel tunnel, then is moved, briefly, to moral feeling:

> The air was light and charming to breathe, free as it was from the impurities that burden the atmosphere near the globe. My spirits rose. It was pleasant to be for the time in a region free from letters, with no post office near, no worries, and above all no telegraphs.

Aboard the *Doña Sol*, 'the Divine Sarah' is in heaven. She finds that up above the clouds there is 'not silence, but the shadow of silence'. She feels the balloon to be 'the emblem of uttermost freedom' – which is also how most groundlings would have viewed the actress herself. Félix Tournachon describes 'the silent immensities of welcoming and beneficent space, where man cannot be reached by any human force or by any power of evil, and where he feels himself live as if for the first time'. In this silent, moral space, the aeronaut experiences health of body and health of soul. Altitude 'reduces all things to their relative proportions, and to the Truth'. Cares, remorse, disgust become strangers: 'How easily indifference, contempt, forgetfulness drop away . . . and forgiveness descends.'

The aeronaut could visit God's space – without the use of magic – and colonise it. And in doing so, he discovered a peace that didn't pass understanding. Height was moral, height was spiritual. Height, some thought, was even political: Victor Hugo believed, quite simply, that heavier-than-air flight would lead to democracy. When *The Giant* crashed near Hanover, Hugo offered to raise a public subscription. Tournachon refused out of pride, so instead the poet composed an open letter in praise of aeronautics. He described walking in the Avenue de l'Observatoire in

Paris with the astronomer François Arago when a balloon launched from the Champ de Mars passed over their heads. Hugo had said to his companion: 'There floats the egg waiting for the bird. But the bird is within and will emerge.' Arago took Hugo's hands and replied ardently, 'And on that day Geo will be called Demos!' Hugo endorsed this 'profound remark', by saying, '"Geo will become Demos." The whole world will be a democracy . . . Man will become bird – and what a bird! A thinking bird. An eagle with a soul!'

This sounds high-flown, overinflated. And aeronautics did not lead to democracy, unless budget airlines count. But aeronautics purged the sin of height, otherwise known as the sin of getting above yourself. Who now had the right to look down on the world from above and command its description? It is time to bring Félix Tournachon into better focus.

He was born in 1820 and died in 1910. He was a tall, gangling figure with a mane of red hair, passionate and restless by nature. Baudelaire called him 'an astonishing expression of vitality'; his gusts of energy and flames of hair seemed enough to lift a balloon into the air by themselves. No one ever accused him of being sensible. The poet Gérard de Nerval introduced him to the magazine editor Alphonse

Karr with the words, 'He is very witty and very stupid.' A later editor and close friend, Charles Philipon, called him 'a man of wit without a shadow of rationality . . . His life has been, still is, and always will be incoherent.' He was the sort of bohemian who lived with his widowed mother until he married; and the sort of husband whose infidelities coexisted with uxoriousness.

He was a journalist, caricaturist, photographer, balloonist, entrepreneur and inventor, a keen registerer of patents and founder of companies; a tireless self-publicist, and in old age a prolific writer of unreliable memoirs. As a progressive, he hated Napoleon III, and sulked in his carriage when the Emperor arrived to watch the departure of *The Giant*. As a photographer, he declined the custom of high society, preferring to memorialise the circles in which he moved; naturally, he photographed Sarah Bernhardt several times. He was an active member of the first French society for the protection of animals. He used to make rude noises at policemen and disapproved of prison (where he had once been confined for debt): he thought juries should ask not 'Is he guilty?' but rather 'Is he dangerous?' He threw huge parties and kept open table; he gave over his studio on the Boulevard des Capucines to the first Impressionist exhibition of 1874. He planned to invent a new sort of gunpowder. He also dreamed of a kind of talking picture, which he called 'an acoustic daguerreotype'. He was hopeless with money.

He was not known by the sturdy Lyonnais name of Tournachon. In the bohemia of his youth, friends were often affectionately rebaptised – for instance, by adding or substituting the suffix -*dar*. So he became first Tournadar, and then simply Nadar. It was as Nadar that he wrote and caricatured and photographed; as Nadar that he became, in the years between 1855 and 1870, the finest portrait photographer yet seen. And this was his name when, in the autumn of 1858, he put together two things that had not been put together before.

Photography, like jazz, was a sudden, contemporary art which achieved technical excellence very quickly. And once it became able to leave the confines of the studio, it tended to spread horizontally, out and across. In 1851 the French government set up the Heliographic Mission, which dispatched five photographers across the land to record the buildings (and ruins) that made up the national patrimony. Two years earlier, it had been a Frenchman who first photographed the Sphinx and the Pyramids. Nadar was less interested in the horizontal than the vertical, in height and depth. His portraits surpass those of his contemporaries because they go deeper. He said that the theory of photography could be learnt in an hour, and its techniques in a day; but what couldn't be taught were a sense of light, a grasp of the moral intelligence of the sitter, and 'the psychological side of photography – the word doesn't seem too ambitious to me'. He relaxed his subjects with chatter, while modelling them with lamps, screens, veils, mirrors and reflectors. The poet Théodore de Banville called him 'a novelist and caricaturist hunting his prey'. It was the novelist who took these psychological portraits, and who concluded that the vainest sitters were actors, closely followed by soldiers. The same novelist also spotted one key difference between the sexes: when a couple who had been jointly photographed returned to examine their proofs, the wife always looked first at the portrait of her husband – and so did the husband. Such was humanity's self-love, Nadar concluded, that most were inevitably disappointed when they finally saw a true image of themselves.

Moral and psychological depth; also physical depth. Nadar was the first to photograph the Paris sewers, where he made twenty-three images. He also descended into the Catacombs, those sewer-like ossuaries where bones were stacked after the cemetery clearances of the 1780s. Here, he needed an eighteen-minute exposure. This was no problem for the dead, of course; but to ape the living, Nadar draped and dressed mannequins, and gave them parts to play — watchman, bone-stacker, labourer pulling a wagon full of skulls and femurs.

And this left height. The things Nadar put together that had not been put together before were two of his three emblems of modernity: photography and aeronautics.

First, a darkroom had to be built in the balloon's cradle, with doubled curtains of black and orange; inside was the merest flicker of a lamp. The new wet-plate technique consisted of coating a glass sheet with collodion, then sensitising it in a solution of silver nitrate. But it was a cumbersome process which required deft handling, so Nadar was accompanied by a plate preparer. The camera was a Dallmeyer, with a special horizontal shutter Nadar had patented. Near Petit-Bicêtre, in the north of Paris, on a day of little wind in the autumn of 1858, the two men made their ascent in a tethered balloon, and took the world's first sky-based photograph. Back down at the local auberge which served as their headquarters, they excitedly developed the plate.

And found nothing. Or rather, nothing but a muddy soot-black expanse with no trace of an image. They tried again, and failed; tried a third time, and failed again. Suspecting that the baths might contain impurities, they filtered and refiltered them, to no effect. They changed all the chemicals, but still it made no difference. Time was passing, winter was approaching, and the great experiment had not worked. Then, as Nadar relates in his memoirs, he was sitting one day beneath an apple tree (a Newtonian coincidence which perhaps stretches credulity), when suddenly he understood the problem. 'The persistent failure derived from the fact that the neck of the balloon, always left open during ascents, allowed hydrosulphuric gas to stream out into my silver baths.' So the next time, once sufficient height had been reached, he closed off the gas valve – a dangerous procedure in itself, which might cause the aerostat to explode. The prepared plate was exposed, and back at the auberge Nadar was rewarded with an image, faint but discernible, of the three buildings beneath the tethered balloon: farm, auberge and gendarmerie. Two white pigeons could be seen on the farm roof; in the lane was a stopped cart, its occupant wondering at the contraption floating in the sky.

This first picture did not survive, except in Nadar's memory and our subsequent imagination; nor did any others he took in the next ten years. The only images of his aerostatic experiments date from 1868. One shows an eight-part, multi-lens view of streets leading to the Arc de Triomphe; another looks across the Avenue du Bois de Boulogne (now Avenue Foch) towards Les Ternes and Montmartre.

On the 23rd of October 1858, Nadar duly took out patent no. 38 509 for 'A new system of aerostatic photography'. But the process proved technically difficult and commercially unprofitable. The lack of public response was also discouraging. He himself imagined two practical applications for his 'new system'. First, it would transform land surveying: from a balloon you could map a million square metres, or a hundred hectares, in one go; and make ten such observations in the course of a day. Its second use would be in military reconnaissance: a balloon could act as a 'travelling church steeple'. This in itself was not new: the Revolutionary Army had used one at the Battle of Fleurus in 1794, while the expeditionary force Napoleon took to Egypt included a Corps d'Aérostation equipped with four balloons (destroyed by Nelson at Aboukir Bay). The addition of photography, however, would clearly give any half-competent general the edge. Yet who should first seek to exploit this possibility? Only the hated Napoleon III, who in 1859 offered Nadar 50,000 francs for his services in the coming war with Austria. The photographer declined.

As for the peacetime use of his patent, Nadar was assured by his 'very eminent friend Colonel Laudesset' that (for reasons unstated) aerial land surveying was 'impossible'. Frustrated, and ever restless, he moved on, leaving the field of aerostatic photography to the Tissandier brothers, to Jacques Ducom, and to his own son, Paul Nadar.

He moved on. During the Prussian siege of Paris, he set up the Compagnie d'Aérostatiers Militaires to provide a communications link to the outside world. Nadar dispatched 'siege balloons' – one of them named the *Victor Hugo*, another the *George Sand* – from the Place St-Pierre in Montmartre, bearing letters, reports to the French government, and intrepid aeronauts. The first flight left on 23 September 1870 and landed safely in Normandy; its postbag contained a letter from Nadar to *The Times* of London, which printed it, in full and in French, five days later. This postal service continued throughout the siege, though some balloons were shot down by the Prussians, and all depended on the wind. One ended up in a Norwegian fjord.

The photographer was always famous: Victor Hugo once addressed an envelope with the single word 'Nadar', and still the letter got to him. In 1862 his friend Daumier caricatured him in a lithograph called *Nadar Raising Photography to the Level of Art*. It depicts him crouched over his camera in the basket of a balloon high above Paris, whose every house is plastered with advertisements for PHOTOGRAPHIE. And if Art was often wary or fearful of Photography, that hustling, arriviste medium, it paid regular, easeful homage to aeronautics. Guardi showed a balloon hovering calmly over Venice; Manet portrayed *The Giant* making its last ascent (with Nadar on board) from Les Invalides. Painters from Goya to Douanier Rousseau made balloons float serenely in a serener sky: the celestial version of pastoral.

But the artist who made the most compelling single image of ballooning was Odilon Redon, and he disagreed. Redon had witnessed *The Giant* in flight, and also Henri Giffard's 'Great Captive Balloon', which starred at the Paris Exhibitions of 1867 and 1878. In the latter year he produced a charcoal drawing called *Eye Balloon*. At first sight it seems just a witty visual pun: the sphere of the balloon and the sphere of the eye are conflated into one, as a vast orb hovers over a grey landscape. The eye balloon has its eyelid open, so that the eyelash makes a fringe round the top of the canopy. Dangling from the balloon is a cradle in which squats a rough hemispherical shape: the top half of a human head. But the tone of the image is new and sinister. We could not be further from ballooning's established tropes: freedom, spiritual exaltation, human progress. Redon's eternally open eye is deeply unsettling. The eye in the sky; God's security camera. And that lumpish human head invites us to conclude that the colonisation of space doesn't purify the colonisers; all that has happened is that we have brought our sinfulness to a new location.

Aeronautics and photography were scientific advances with practical civic consequences. And yet, in their early years, an aura of mystery and magic surrounded each of them. Those bug-eyed yokels running after the trailing anchor of a balloon might have expected Simon Magus to descend from it just as much as Sarah the Divine. And photography seemed to threaten more than just a sitter's *amour propre*. It wasn't only forest dwellers who feared that the camera might steal their soul. Nadar recalled that Balzac had a theory of the self, according to which a person's essence was made up of a near-infinite series of spectral layers, one superimposed on the next. The novelist further believed that during the 'Daguerrean operation' one such layer was stripped away and retained by the magic instrument. Nadar couldn't remember if this layer was supposedly lost for ever, or whether regeneration was possible; though he cheekily suggested that, given Balzac's corpulence, he had less to fear than most from having a few spectral layers removed. But this theory – or apprehension – wasn't unique to Balzac. It was shared by his writer friends Gautier and Nerval, making up what Nadar termed a 'cabbalistic trio'.

Félix Tournachon was an uxorious man. He had married Ernestine in September 1854. It was a sudden wedding which surprised his friends: the bride was an eighteen-year-old from the Protestant bourgeoisie of Normandy. True, she had a dowry; and marriage was a useful way for Félix of escaping Life with Mother. But for all his divagations, the relationship appears to have been as tender as it was long. Tournachon quarrelled with his only brother and his only son; both were written – or wrote themselves – out of his life. Ernestine was always there. If there was a pattern to his life, she provided it. She was with him at the crash of *The Giant* near Hanover. Her money helped pay for his studio; later, the business was put in her name.

In 1887, hearing of a fire at the Opéra Comique, and believing her son Paul to be there, Ernestine suffered a stroke. Félix immediately moved the household out of Paris to the Forest of Sénart, where he owned a property called L'Hermitage. They stayed there for the next eight years. In 1893 Edmond de Goncourt described the ménage in his *Journal*:

. . . At its centre is Mme Nadar, aphasiac, looking
like an old white-haired professor. She is lying down,
wrapped in a sky-blue dressing gown lined with pink
silk. Next to her, Nadar takes the part of the tender
nurse, tucking her brightly coloured gown around her,
easing the hair off her temples, touching and stroking
her all the time.

Her dressing gown is *bleu de ciel*, the colour of the sky in
which they no longer flew. Both were grounded now. In 1909,
after fifty-five years of marriage, Ernestine died. That same
year, Louis Blériot flew the Channel, a final endorsement of
Nadar's belief in heavier-than-air flight; the balloonist sent
the aviator a telegram of congratulations. While Blériot
went up into the air, Ernestine went down into the ground.
While Blériot flew, Nadar had lost his rudder. He did not
survive Ernestine long; he died in March 1910, surrounded
by his dogs and cats.

By now, few remembered his achievement at Petit-Bicêtre
in the autumn of 1858. And the aerostatic photographs
that exist are of only passable quality: we must imagine
the excitement back into them. But they represent a
moment when the world grew up. Or perhaps that is
too melodramatic, and too hopeful. Perhaps the world

progresses not by maturing, but by being in a permanent state of adolescence, of thrilled discovery. Still, this was an instant of cognitive change. The vestigial human outline on a cave wall, the first mirror, the development of portraiture, the science of photography – these were advances which allowed us to look at ourselves better, with increasing truth. And even if the world was largely unaware at the time of events at Petit-Bicêtre, the change could not be unchanged, unmade. And the sin of height was purged.

Once, the peasant had looked up at the heavens, where God lived, fearing thunder, hail, and God's anger, hoping for sun, a rainbow, and God's approval. Now, the modern peasant looked up at the heavens and saw instead the less daunting arrival of Colonel Fred Burnaby, cigar in one pocket and half-sovereign in the other, of Sarah Bernhardt and her autobiographical chair, of Félix Tournachon in his airborne wicker cottage, complete with refreshment room, lavatory and photographic department.

Nadar's only surviving aerostatic photographs date from 1868. Exactly a century later, in December 1968, the *Apollo 8* mission lifted off for its journey to the moon. On Christmas Eve, the spacecraft passed behind the far side of the moon and entered lunar orbit. As it emerged, the astronauts were the first humans to see a phenomenon for which a new word was needed: 'earthrise'. The pilot of the lunar module, William Anders, using a specially adapted Hasselblad camera, photographed a two-thirds-full Earth soaring in a night sky. His pictures show it in luscious colour, with feathery cloud cover, swirling storm systems, rich blue seas and rusty continents. Major General Anders later reflected:

> I think it was the Earthrise that really kind of got everybody in the solar plexus . . . We were looking back at our planet, the place where we evolved. Our Earth was quite colorful, pretty and delicate compared to the very rough, rugged, beat-up, even boring lunar surface. I think it struck everybody that here we'd come 240,000 miles to see the Moon and it was the Earth that was really worth looking at.

At the time, Anders's photos were as disturbing as they were beautiful; and they remain so today. To look at ourselves from afar, to make the subjective suddenly objective: this gives us a psychic shock. But it was the flame-haired Félix Tournachon — if only from a height of a few hundred metres, if only in black and white, if only in a few local views of Paris — who first put two things together.

ON THE LEVEL

You put together two things that have not been put together before; and sometimes it works, sometimes it doesn't. Pilâtre de Rozier, the first man to ascend in a fire balloon, also planned to be the first to fly the Channel from France to England. To this end he constructed a new kind of aerostat, with a hydrogen balloon on top, to give greater lift, and a fire balloon beneath, to give better control. He put these two things together, and on the 15th of June 1785, when the winds seemed favourable, he made his ascent from the Pas-de-Calais. The brave new contraption rose swiftly, but before it had even reached the coastline, flame appeared at the top of the hydrogen balloon, and the whole, hopeful aerostat, now looking to one observer like a heavenly gas lamp, fell to earth, killing both pilot and co-pilot.

You put together two people who have not been put together before; and sometimes the world is changed, sometimes not. They may crash and burn, or burn and crash. But sometimes, something new is made, and then the world is changed. Together, in that first exaltation, that first roaring sense of uplift, they are greater than their two separate selves. Together, they see further, and they see more clearly.

Of course, love may not be evenly matched; perhaps it rarely is. To put it another way: how did those besieged Parisians of 1870–71 get replies to their letters? You can fly a balloon out from the Place St-Pierre and assume it will land somewhere useful; but you can hardly expect the winds, however patriotic, to blow it back to Montmartre on a return flight. Various stratagems were proposed: for example, placing the return correspondence in large metal globes and floating them downstream into the city, there to be caught in nets. Pigeon post was a more obvious idea, and a Batignolles pigeon fancier put his dovecote at the authorities' disposal: a basket of birds might be flown out with each siege balloon, and return bearing letters. But compare the freight capacity of a balloon and a pigeon, and imagine the weight of disappointment. According to Nadar, the solution came from an engineer who worked in sugar manufacture. Letters intended for Paris were to be written in a clear hand, on one side of the paper, with the recipient's address at the top. Then, at the collecting station, hundreds of them would be laid side by side on a large screen and photographed. The image would be micrographically reduced, flown into Paris by carrier pigeon, and enlarged back to readable size. The revived letters were then put into envelopes and delivered to their addressees. It was better than nothing; indeed, it was a technical triumph. But imagine a pair of lovers, one able to write privately and at length on both sides of the page, and hide the tenderest words in an envelope; the other constrained by brevity and the knowledge that private feelings might be publicly inspected by photographers and postmen. Although – isn't that how love sometimes feels, and works?

Sarah Bernhardt was photographed by Nadar – first the father, later the son – throughout her life. Her first session took place when she was about twenty, at the time Félix Tournachon was also involved in another tumultuous, if briefer, career: that of *The Giant*. Sarah is not yet Divine – she is unknown, aspiring; yet the portraits already show her a star. She is simply posed, wrapped in a velvet cloak, or an enveloping shawl. Her shoulders are bare; she wears no jewellery except a small pair of cameo earrings; her hair is virtually undressed. So is she: there is more than a hint that she wears little beneath that cloak, that shawl. Her expression is withholding, and thus alluring. She is, of course, very beautiful, perhaps more so to the modern eye than at the time. She seems to embody truthfulness, theatricality and mystery – and make those abstractions compatible. Nadar also took a nude photograph which some claim is of her. It shows a woman, naked to the waist, peek-a-booing with one eye from behind a spread fan. Whatever the case, the portraits of Sarah cloaked and shawled are decidedly more erotic.

Scarcely five feet tall, she was not considered the right size for an actress; also, too pale and too thin. She seemed impulsive and natural in both life and art; she broke theatrical rules, often turning upstage to deliver a speech. She slept with all her leading men. She loved fame and self-publicity – or, as Henry James silkily put it, she was 'a figure so admirably suited for conspicuity'. One critic compared her successively to a Russian princess, a Byzantine empress and a Muscat begum, before concluding: 'Above all, she is as Slav as one can be. She is much more Slav than all the Slavs I have ever met.' In her early twenties she had an illegitimate son, whom she took everywhere with her, heedless of disapproval. She was Jewish in a largely anti-Semitic France, while in Catholic Montreal they stoned her carriage. She was brave and doughty.

Naturally, she had enemies. Her success, her sex, her racial origin and her bohemian extravagance reminded the puritanical why actors used to be buried in unhallowed ground. And over the decades her acting style, once so original, inevitably dated, since naturalness onstage is just as much an artifice as naturalism in the novel. If the magic always worked for some – Ellen Terry called her 'transparent as an azalea' and compared her stage presence to 'smoke from a burning paper' – others were less kind. Turgenev, though a Francophile and himself a dramatist, found her 'false, cold, affected', and condemned her 'repulsive Parisian chic'.

Fred Burnaby was often described as bohemian. His official biographer wrote that he lived 'entirely aloof, absolutely regardless of conventionalities'. And he had known the exoticism which Bernhardt merely appropriated. A traveller might bring reports back to Paris from afar; a playwright would pillage them for themes and effects; then a designer and costumier would perfect the illusion around her. Burnaby had been that traveller: he had gone deep into Russia, across Asia Minor and the Middle East, up the Nile. He had crossed Fashoda country, where both sexes went naked and dyed their hair bright yellow. Stories that adhered to him often featured Circassian girls, gypsy dancers and pretty Kirghiz widows.

He claimed descent from Edward I, the king known as Longshanks, and displayed virtues of courage and truth-speaking which the English imagine unique to themselves. Yet there was something unsettling about him. His father was said to be 'melancholy as the padge-owl that hooted in his park', and Fred, though vigorous and extrovert, inherited this trait. He was enormously strong, yet frequently ill, tormented by liver and stomach pains; 'gastric catarrh' once drove him to a foreign spa. And though 'very popular in London and Paris', and a member of the Prince of Wales's circle, he was described by the *Dictionary of National Biography* as living 'much alone'.

The conventional accept and are frequently charmed by a certain unconventionality; Burnaby seems to have exceeded that limit. One of his devoted friends called him 'the most slovenly rascal that ever lived', who sat 'like a sack of corn on a horse'. He was held to be foreign-looking, with 'oriental features' and a Mephistophelean smile. The *DNB* called his looks 'Jewish and Italian', noting that his 'unEnglish' appearance 'led him to resist attempts to procure portraits of him'.

We live on the flat, on the level, and yet – and so – we aspire. Groundlings, we can sometimes reach as far as the gods. Some soar with art, others with religion; most with love. But when we soar, we can also crash. There are few soft landings. We may find ourselves bouncing across the ground with leg-fracturing force, dragged towards some foreign railway line. Every love story is a potential grief story. If not at first, then later. If not for one, then for the other. Sometimes, for both.

So why do we constantly aspire to love? Because love is the meeting point of truth and magic. Truth, as in photography; magic, as in ballooning.

Despite Burnaby's reticence and Bernhardt's waywardness with fact, we may establish that they met in Paris in the mid-1870s. It was not difficult for an intimate of the Prince of Wales to gain access to the Divine Sarah. He sent flowers beforehand, watched her in Bornier's *La Fille de Roland*, prepared his words of praise, and went round afterwards. He was half expecting a *cohue* of effete Parisian dandies in her dressing room, but perhaps some preliminary triage had taken place. He was comfortably the tallest person there, she the tiniest. When she greeted him, he could not help mentioning how the stage enlarged her. She was used to such a reaction.

'And so thin,' she added, 'that I can slip between rain-drops without getting wet.'

Fred looked as if he almost believed her. She laughed a little, but without any mockery. He felt at ease. In truth, he felt at ease in most places. He was an Englishman, for a start; he spoke seven languages excellently; while any officer used to giving orders from Spain to Russian Turkestan was well able to cut it among these effusive yet genial gallants who, as it appeared to him, were competing with one another only in flights of language.

They were drinking champagne, no doubt provided by one of these admirers. Fred was always temperate with wine, and so able to observe discreet departures until, it suddenly seemed, there was only a duenna by the name of Mme Guérard to prevent him being alone with her.

'So, *mon capitaine —*'

'Oh, for pity's sake, ma'am. Fred. Or Frederick. When I enter your dressing room I am without rank. I am . . .' He hesitated. 'I am, as you might say, a simple soldier.'

He felt, rather than watched, her examine his walking-out dress: stable jacket, cavalry overalls, ankle boots, spurs; forage cap temporarily abandoned on a side table.

'And what is your war?' she asked smilingly.

He didn't know how to reply. He thought about wars, where only men were employed. He thought about sieges, and how men were supposed to besiege women until they surrendered. But for once he did not feel bravado, and he was often uneasy with metaphor. Eventually, he replied:

'Not so long ago, ma'am, I was returning from Odessa. News had reached me that my father was ill. The quickest route lay through Paris. But the city was in the hands of the Commune.' He paused, wondering what the actress's view of that pestiferous gang of assassins might be. 'I had only my travelling bag and regulation cavalry sword. I was warned that all weapons were forbidden. But I have long shanks, and so I hid my sword down the leg of my trousers.'

He paused, long enough for her to think this the end of the story.

'So I limped. And I was pretty soon arrested by an officer of the Commune, who was rightly suspicious of the stiffness of my leg. He charged me with carrying a concealed weapon. I immediately acknowledged the offence, but informed him that I was returning to visit my sick father, and that I only sought peace. Rather to my surprise, he allowed me to continue on my journey.'

Now the story did seem to have ended, but its point eluded her.

'And how was your father?'

'Oh, he was much restored by the time I reached Somerby. Thank you for your consideration. The point of the story — well, to repeat what I told the fellow who arrested me, in Paris I only seek peace.'

She looked at him, at this enormous, uniformed, moustachioed, francophone Englishman, whose thin, piercing voice came strangely out of a vast body. And since she lived her life amid complication and artifice, simplicity always moved her.

'I am touched, Capitaine Fred. But – how can I put it? I am myself not yet ready for a quiet life.'

Now he was embarrassed. Had she taken his remark amiss?

'You will come back tomorrow,' said Sarah Bernhardt.

'I shall come back tomorrow,' replied Fred Burnaby, giving her a farewell of his own devising: a military self-dismissal combined with a bohemian's eager promise to return.

The women she played were passionate, exotic, operatic – literally so. She created Dumas's *La Dame aux Camélias* before Verdi reimagined it; and was Sardou's La Tosca, a role now only known in Puccini's version. She was operatic without needing music. She had a ménage of lovers and a menagerie of animals. The lovers seemed to get on with one another, perhaps because there was safety in numbers; also because she was good at turning them into friends. She once said that if she died prematurely, her admirers would still continue to gather regularly at her house. This was probably true.

Her menagerie had begun humbly enough, when she was a girl, with a pair of goats and a blackbird. Later, the wildlife became wilder. On tour in England, she bought a cheetah, seven chameleons and a wolf dog in Liverpool. There was Darwin the monkey, Hernani II the lion cub, and dogs called Cassis and Vermouth. In New Orleans she bought an alligator which reacted to its French diet of milk and champagne by dying. She also had a boa constrictor which ate sofa cushions and had to be shot – by Sarah herself.

Fred Burnaby was not abashed by such a creature.

The next evening, he watched her performance, came to her dressing room, and saw many of the same faces. He made sure to pay proper attention to Mme Guérard: having been in foreign courts before, he knew to recognise the power behind the throne. Soon – much sooner than the fiercest optimism could have imagined – she came across, took Burnaby's arm, and bade her coterie goodnight. As the three of them left, the scrimmage of Parisian dandies took care not to appear put out. Well, perhaps they weren't.

They rode in her carriage to her house in the rue Fortuny. The table was laid, the champagne on ice, and through a half-open door Fred glimpsed the corner of an enormous cane bed. Mme Guérard retired. If there were servants, he did not see them; if there were parrots or lion cubs around, he did not hear them. He heard only her voice, which had the clarity and range of a musical instrument yet to be invented.

He told her of his travels, his military skirmishing, his balloon adventures. He spoke of his ambition to fly across the German Ocean.

'Why not the Channel?' she asked, almost as if it were uncivil of him, wanting to fly in any direction other than towards her.

'That has also been my ambition. But the winds are the problem, ma'am.'

'Sarah.'

'Madame Sarah.' Stolidly, he continued: 'The fact of the matter is, that if you take off from almost anywhere in southern England, you generally find yourself landing in Essex.'

'What is this Essex?'

'You do not need to know. It is not exotic, Essex.'

She looked at him a little uncertainly. Was this a fact or a joke?

'A southerly, a south-westerly takes you to Essex. You need a good constant blowing westerly to get you across the German Ocean. But to reach France, you would need a northerly, which is somewhat rare and unreliable.'

'So you will not visit me by balloon?' she asked flirtatiously.

'Madame Sarah, I would visit you by any means of transportation now or yet to be invented, were you in Paris or in Timbuctoo.' He startled himself with this sudden gust of declaration, and took more cold pheasant as if it were a matter of urgency. 'But I have a theory,' he continued, a little more calmly. 'I am convinced that the winds do not always blow in the same direction at different heights. So if you were caught in . . . in a contrary wind . . .'

'An Essex wind?'

'Precisely – if you were so caught, you would release ballast and seek the higher altitudes where that northerly might be found.'

'And if it is not?'

'Then you would end up in the water.'

'But you know how to swim?'

'Yes, but it would do me little good. There are some balloonists who wear cork overjackets in case they land in the sea. But that strikes me as unsporting. I believe a man should take his chances.'

She left that remark hanging in the air.

The next day, all that stopped him from feeling pure exultance was the question: had it been too easy? In Seville, he had spent many hours learning the language of the fan from a solemn Andalusian señorita: what this gesture, that concealment, this tap really meant. He understood and had practised gallantry on more than one continent, and found much charm in female coquetry. What he had not come across before was such straightforwardness, the acknowledgement of appetite and the unwillingness to waste time. He knew, of course, that all was not entirely straightforward. Fred Burnaby was not so naive as to imagine that he was being entertained merely for the attraction of his person. He realised that Madame Sarah was no different from other actresses, and that presents were expected. And since Madame Sarah was the greatest actress of her day, the presents must be similarly resplendent.

Burnaby had previously been in full charge of his flirtations: the girl, nervous of the vast uniform in front of her, would need calming. Now, things were the other way round, which both perplexed and excited him. There was no shilly-shallying about rendezvous. He would ask, she would grant. Sometimes they met at the theatre, sometimes he came directly to the rue Fortuny, a place which – now he had time to examine it – struck him as half mansion, half artist's studio. There were velvet-clad walls, parrots perching on portrait busts, vases as big as sentry boxes, and as many soaring and drooping plants as at Kew. And among such riot and display lay those simple things the heart desired: dinner, and bed, and sleep, and breakfast. A man scarcely dared ask for more. He could hear himself living.

She told him about her early life, her struggles, her

ambition and her success. And about all the rivalry and jealousy that success provoked.

'They say terrible things about me, Capitaine Fred. They say that I roast cats and eat their fur. That I dine off lizards' tails and the brains of peacocks sautéed in butter made from monkeys. They say that I play croquet with human skulls wrapped in Louis Quatorze wigs.'

'I can't see the sport in that,' commented Burnaby, frowning.

'But enough of my life. Tell me more about your balloons,' she asked.

He pondered. Lead with the ace, he thought. Best foot forward, best story forward.

'Last year,' he began, 'I made an ascent from the Crystal Palace with Mr Lucy and Captain Colvile. The wind was moving between southerly and westerly and back again. We were above the cloud, and our guess was that we were probably crossing the estuary of the Thames. The sun was full above us, and as the captain correctly observed, it was confoundedly hot. So I took off my coat and hung it on one of the spikes of the anchor, and replied to him that there was at least one comfort in being above the clouds. Namely, that a gentleman could sit in public in his shirtsleeves.'

He paused and laughed, expecting laughter in return, as

in London, but she had a small smile on her face, and a quizzing look. Alarmed by her silence, he pressed on.

'But then, you see, as we were sitting there, with so little wind that we felt almost becalmed, we dropped our eyes — well, one of us did, and then alerted the others — downwards. Imagine the scene. There was a broad expanse of fleecy cloud beneath us, preventing our view of the land, or the estuary, below, and then, there, we saw an amazing sight. The sun' — he held up a hand to indicate its position — 'was casting on to this flat surface of cloud the very shape and shadow of our balloon. We could see the gasbag, the ropes, the cradle and, strangest of all, our three heads clearly outlined. It was as if we were looking at a colossal photograph of ourselves, of our expedition.'

'Larger than life.'

'Indeed.' But Fred was aware that he had rather garbled his story. The strength of her attention had panicked him. He felt deflated.

'As we both are. I am larger than life on the stage, as you yourself remarked. And you are larger than life in your very being.'

Fred sensed a pull and lift in his heart. He had deserved censure and received praise. He enjoyed flattery as much as the next man — but again, her words struck him as mere straightforwardness. And here was the paradox of their situation. They were each, by the standards of conventional life, exotic beings, and yet when they were together he discerned no play, no acting, no costume. Even though he was in the walking-out dress of the Blues, and she had only just cast aside furs and a hat which appeared to have a dead owl roosting in it. He was, he admitted, half confused and probably three-quarters in love.

'If ever I take a balloon flight,' she said, with a slight, faraway smile, 'I shall think of you. I promise you that. And I always keep my promises.'

'Always?'

'Always if I intend to. Of course there are promises I do not intend to keep when I make them. But those are hardly promises, are they?'

'Then perhaps you might honour me by promising to make an ascent with me one day?'

She paused. Had he gone too far? But what was the use of straightforwardness, if not saying what you mean, what you feel?

'But Capitaine Fred, might it not be a little difficult to balance the vessel?'

This was a good practical point: he weighed at least twice as much as she did. They would have to put most of the ballast on her side, but if he then had to cross the basket in order to release it . . . He was imagining the playlet as if it were real, and only later began to wonder if she was talking of other things. But then, metaphor often confused him.

No, he wasn't three-quarters in love.

'Hook, line and sinker,' he said to his uniformed reflection in the cheval glass of his hotel bedroom. The dull gold of its frame yielded to the brighter lace edgings of his stable jacket. 'Hook, line and sinker, Captain Fred.'

He had often imagined this moment, tried to see how it would compare with those previous times when he had been only half in love – with a pair of eyes, a smile, the shimmer of a dress. On those occasions he had always been able to picture the next few days – and sometimes those next few days had turned out exactly as he had predicted. But then, the imagination and the actuality had stopped; the dream and the desire had been fulfilled. Now, though the desire had, in one sense, been fulfilled sooner and more giddyingly than he could possibly have dreamed, it merely aroused greater desire. The small time he had spent with her aroused the desire for greater time, for all time. The small distance they had travelled from the theatre to the rue Fortuny aroused a desire to travel greater distances: to all those countries whose inhabitants she had portrayed on-stage – and then to all the remaining countries in the world. To go everywhere with her. Someone had remarked to him upon her Slav beauty. And so he imagined travelling east with her, comparing her features with those around them until she blended entirely into the physiognomical scenery, and there was nothing left but a sea of Slavs and Captain Fred. He imagined her tiny, lithe figure at his side, on a horse she would mount not woman-fashion but astride, in another trouser role. He saw them sharing a horse, he behind, she in front, enclosed by his arms as he held the reins.

He saw them as a couple, putting things together, assembling a life. He always imagined them in motion. He was – they were – soaring.

Though bohemian, and worldly, Fred Burnaby was not sophisticated in the manner of those who came backstage each night and sought ever more refined ways to applaud. But he was intelligent, and had travelled widely. So, after a week or two, awareness came of how others might view his situation; and he spoke their words aloud to himself.

'She is a woman. She is French. She is an actress. Is she on the level?'

He knew what his friends and fellow officers would say. How they would smirk even as he articulated the question. But their minds would be filled with generality, reputation, rumour. They themselves were perfectly happy chasing Circassian girls and pretty Kirghiz widows for a while, secure in the knowledge that they would return home and marry Englishwomen of good family for whom the practicalities of the heart were no more complicated and mysterious than the practicalities of the kitchen garden. Late at night, over a brandy and soda, they might briefly succumb to nostalgia for a different kind of smile, a darker complexion, and some whispered words in a half-understood language. But then, having done so, they would dutifully go back to the family hearth, squiffily convinced that they had ordered their lives properly.

Fred Burnaby was not like this. And neither was Madame Sarah. She had not used flirtatiousness with him. Or rather, her flirtatiousness was not a fraud, not a tactic, but a promise. Her eyes and her smile had been a proposal, an offer which he had accepted. The fact that Mme Guérard had subsequently mentioned a pair of earrings to which Madame Sarah had taken a fancy, that he had bought them for her, and that she had expressed gratitude but no surprise: this too was straightforwardness. And to his mocking fellow officers he would reply: but did you not equally buy presents for your virginal rose-cheeked English fiancées, and did they not accept them with such a pretty affectation of astonishment that you were quite deceived? Whereas Madame Sarah had always – even though 'always' meant only a few weeks – been straight with him.

She did not have a suspicious family with whom he had to ingratiate himself. There was Mme Guérard: vanguard, rearguard and *état-major* all combined. He recognised and appreciated loyalty. She and Captain Fred understood one another; and when events spurred him to generosity, she took his money with a calm gravity. Otherwise, there was only Madame Sarah's son, a friendly lad who might successfully be taught sports and games. The Continentals still needed such an education in these matters. In Spain they were proud to shoot a sitting partridge. At Pau he had once been invited to join the local hunt. They had used a bagged fox doused in aniseed to make it easier for the dull-nosed hounds to follow; his horse was so abbreviated that his heels dragged the ground as it carried him; and the whole sport was over in a mere twenty minutes.

He would happily quit England. He had known good fellowship there, but his soul was drawn to heat and dust. And though his blood might be pure English all the way back to Edward Longshanks, he was aware that it did not always show. He knew what some privately thought, because in drink they nearly said it to his face. When he was a young subaltern, there had been a joke in the mess that he looked like an Italian baritone. 'Sing us a song, Burnaby,' the fellows would chant. And so, every time, until they tired of it, he would stand and sing them neither operetta nor bawdy, but some plain, lilting song of the English shires.

And there had been that supercilious young lieutenant called Dyer, always suggesting he might be a Jew. Not in so many words, of course, just the broadest hints. 'Money? Let's ask Burnaby about that.' Not so subtle. After a few such remarks, he had taken Lieutenant Dyer aside and spoken as if they were not wearing uniform. And that had been the end of it. But Burnaby did remember.

So the fact that Madame Sarah had been born a Jewess was not of great concern to him. Born a Jewess, converted to Catholicism. Burnaby did not absolve himself of strong feelings when it came to preferring one race over another, but he did believe that in the matter of the Jews, he looked on them more benignly than did most Frenchmen he had met. So, in a way, he took such prejudice upon himself, and Dyer might consider them both false Jews if he wanted to. Which made him feel closer to Madame Sarah.

And so, as the weeks passed, he imagined their future more precisely. He would resign his commission. He would quit England, and she would quit Paris. Of course, she would continue to amaze the world, but her genius must not be squandered day after day, night after night. She would play a season here, a season there, and in between they would travel to places where she was as yet unknown. From their shared bohemianism, a new pattern would emerge. Love would change her, as it was changing him. How, he did not exactly know.

So that was all clear in his mind, and he must bring the subject up. Not now, of course, not between dinner and bed. It was a matter for the morning. High-hearted, he addressed himself to the ballotine of duck.

'Capitaine Fred,' she began, and he thought that his definition of bliss would be to hear those two words, in that voice, in that French accent, for the rest of his days. 'Capitaine Fred, what do you imagine to be the future of flight? Of human flight, human beings, men and women, up in the atmosphere together?'

He answered the question he heard.

'Aerial navigation is a mere question of lightness and force,' he replied. 'Attempts – my own included – to propel and steer balloons have failed. And probably will continue to do so. There is no doubt that heavier-than-air flight is the future.'

'I see. I have not yet ascended in a balloon, but I think that a pity.'

He cleared his throat.

'May I ask why, my dear?'

'Of course, Capitaine Fred. Ballooning is freedom, is it not?'

'Indeed.'

'It is being blown whichever way by nature's whims. It is dangerous too.'

'Indeed.'

'Whereas, if we are to imagine a heavier-than-air machine, it would be equipped with some kind of engine. It would have controls by which it might be steered, which would order its ascent and descent. And it would be less dangerous.'

'Undoubtedly.'

'Do you not see what I am saying?'

Burnaby reflected. Was it because she was a woman, because she was French, or because she was an actress, that he did not understand?

'I fear I am still in the clouds, Madame Sarah.'

She smiled again, and not an actress's smile – unless, he suddenly realised, an actress would, as a normal part of her skills, have a non-actress's smile at her disposal.

'I do not say that war is preferable to peace. I do not say that. But danger is preferable to safety.'

Now he thought he might be on to her meaning, and did not like the sound of it.

'I believe in danger as much as you. That will never leave me. I shall always go where danger and adventure call. I shall always seek a skirmish. If my country needs me, I shall always answer.'

'I am happy to know that.'

'But . . .'

'But?'

'Madame Sarah, the future lies with heavier-than-air machines. However much we balloonatics might prefer it not to.'

'Have we not discussed this and agreed?'

'Yes. But that is not what I intended.'

He paused. She waited. He knew that she knew where he was going. He began again.

'We are both bohemians. Both travellers, footloose. We live against the common run of things. We do not take orders easily.'

He paused, she waited.

'Oh, for God's sake, Madame Sarah. You know what I am going to say. I cannot bandy metaphor any longer. I am not the first man who has fallen in love with you on sight, nor, I fear, will I be the last. But I am in love with you as I have never been before. We are kindred spirits, this I know.'

He gazed at her. She looked back at him with what he took to be perfect tranquillity. But did that mean she agreed with him, or was unmoved by what he said? He went on.

'We are both grown up. We know the world. I am not some parlour soldier. You are not an ingénue. Marry me.

Marry me. I lay my sword at your feet as well as my heart. I cannot say it more straightforwardly than that.'

He waited for her response. He thought her eyes glistened. She put her hand on his arm.

'*Mon cher* Capitaine Fred,' she replied – but her tone made him feel more like a schoolboy than an officer of the Blues. 'I have never taken you for a parlour soldier. I do you the honour of taking you seriously. And I am very flattered.'

'But . . . ?'

'But. Yes, that is a word life forces upon us more often than we want, more often than we imagine. But – I do you the honour of answering your straightforwardness with mine. But – I am not made for happiness.'

'You cannot say, after these last weeks and months . . .'

'Oh, but I can say. And I do. I am made for sensation, for pleasure, for the moment. I am constantly in search of new sensations, new emotions. That is how I shall be until my life is worn away. My heart desires more excitement than anyone – any one person – can give.'

He looked away from her. This was more than a man could bear.

'You must understand this,' she went on. 'I shall never marry. I promise you that. I shall always be, as you put it, a balloonatic. I shall never take that heavier-than-air machine with anyone. What can I do? You must not be angry with me. You must think of me as an incomplete person.'

He summoned up one last attempt. 'Madame Sarah, we are all of us incomplete. I am just as incomplete as you. That is why we seek another person. For completion. And I too have never thought I would marry. Not because it is the conventional thing to do. But because I previously did not have the courage. Marriage is a greater danger than a pack of infidels with spears, if you want my opinion. Do not be afraid, Madame Sarah. Do not let your actions be governed by your fears. That is what my first commanding officer used to tell me.'

'It is not fear, Capitaine Fred,' she said gently. 'It is self-knowledge. And do not be angry with me.'

'I am not angry. You have a manner which quite disarms anger. If I appear angry, it is because I am angry with the universe that has made you, that has made us, so that this . . . so that this is how . . .'

'Capitaine Fred. It is late, and we are both tired. Come to my dressing room tomorrow and perhaps you will understand.'

(In parenthesis, another love story. In 1893 – the same year he visits Nadar and his aphasiac wife in the Forest of Sénart – Edmond de Goncourt dines with Sarah Bernhardt before a read-through of his play *La Faustin*. She is still out at rehearsal when he arrives, and he is shown into the studio where she receives her guests. His aesthete's eye chillingly evaluates the tumultuous decor. He finds it a terrible mishmash of medieval sideboards and marquetry cabinets, Chilean figurines and primitive musical instruments, and 'flashy wog objets d'art'. The only sign of authentic personal taste is an array of polar-bear skins in the corner where Bernhardt (who often, as this evening, dresses in white) likes to hold court. Amid such artistic rag-and-bonery, Goncourt also notices a small but intense emotional drama. In the middle of the studio is a cage containing a tiny monkey and a parrot with an enormous bill. The monkey is a whirr of motion, zipping around on the trapeze, and constantly tormenting the parrot, pulling out its feathers and 'martyrising' it. And though the parrot could easily cut the monkey in half with its beak, it does nothing but utter plaintive, heart-rending cries. Goncourt feels sorry for the poor parrot, and comments on the dreadful life it is forced to endure. Whereupon it is explained to him that bird and beast had once been separated, but that the parrot had almost died of grief. It only recovered after being put back into the cage with its tormentor.)

He sent flowers ahead. He watched her impersonate

Adrienne Lecouvreur, that actress of a previous century, poisoned by a love rival. He went to her dressing room. She was charming. There were the usual faces. They spoke in the usual way, muttered the usual opinions. He sat with Mme Guérard, discreetly quizzing her, trying to find some new tactic, some hidden fulcrum . . . when there was a slight hush, and he looked up. He saw her on the arm of a stunted little Frenchman with a monkey face and a stupid cane.

'Goodnight, gentlemen.'

In reply, there was a murmur of complicit unsurprise, exactly as there had been on his own first evening with her. She looked across at him and nodded, then calmly switched her gaze. Mme Guérard rose and bade him goodnight. He watched Madame Sarah depart. He had been given his answer. The water was freezing and he had not so much as a cork overjacket to protect him.

No, he was not angry. And the dressing-room dandies at least had the good breeding not to draw attention to what had happened, nor to imply that something similar – no, precisely the same – had befallen them on previous occasions. They offered him more champagne and asked politely about *le Prince de Galles*. They kept their propriety and respected his. In this, at least, he could not fault them.

But he would never join their number, never be a member of the smiling retinue of former lovers. He considered that sort of behaviour rather beastly, in fact immoral. He refused to be turned from a lover into a dear friend. He was uninterested in that transition. Nor would he club together with others of the same status to buy her some new exotic gift – a snow leopard, perhaps. And he was not angry. But, before the pain set in, he had the time to be rueful. He had laid everything out, the best of himself, and it had not been enough. He had considered himself a bohemian, but she had proved too bohemian for him. And he had failed to understand her explanation of herself.

The pain was to last several years. He eased it by travelling and skirmishing. He never talked about it. If someone enquired into his black mood, he would reply that the melancholy of the padge-owl was afflicting him. The enquirer would understand, and ask no more.

Had he been naive, or overambitious? Both, probably. In life, you might be a bohemian and an adventurer, but you also sought a pattern, an arrangement to help you through, even if – even as – you kicked against it. Army regulations gave you this. But elsewhere: how could a man tell which was a true pattern and which a false? This was one question which pursued him. Here was another: had she been on the level? Had she been natural, or feigning naturalness? Constantly he went back over the evidence of his memories. She had said that she always kept her promises – unless she didn't mean to keep them in the first place. Had she made him false promises? None that he could pin down. Had she told him that she loved him? Yes, of course, many times; but it was his imagination – the prompter's voice at his ear – which had added the words 'for ever'. He hadn't asked what she meant when she told him she loved him. What lover ever does? Those plush and gilded words rarely seem to need annotation at the time.

And now he realised that if he had asked her, she would have replied, 'I shall love you for as long as I shall love you.' What lover could ask for more? And the prompter's voice would again have whispered, 'Which means for ever.' Such was the measure of a man's vanity. Was their love, then, merely the construction of his fancy? That he could not, did not believe. He had loved her as much as he was able for three months, and she had done the same; it was just that her love had a timing switch built into it. Nor would it have helped to ask about her previous lovers, and how long they had lasted. Because their very failure, their impermanence, would only have seemed to promise his success: that is what every lover believes.

No, Fred Burnaby concluded, she had been on the level. It was he who had deceived himself. But if being on the level didn't shield you from pain, maybe it was better to be up in the clouds.

He never tried to make contact with Madame Sarah again. When she came to London he found reason to be out of town. After a while he became able to read of her latest triumph with a steady eye. Mostly, he could go back over the whole business like a rational man, to remember it as something that had happened, that was nobody's fault, that had not involved cruelty, merely misunderstanding. But he could not always hold on to such calmness and such explanations. And then he saw himself as the stupidest of animals. He felt like that boa constrictor which had taken upon itself to start eating sofa cushions, until it had been shot dead by Madame Sarah's own hand. Shot dead, that was how he felt.

But he was to marry, at the advanced age of thirty-seven. She was Elizabeth Hawkins-Whitsed, daughter of an Irish baronet. Yet if he sought, or expected, a pattern, it was again denied him. After the wedding, the bride went down with consumption, and their North African honeymoon was relocated to a Swiss sanatorium. Eleven months later, Elizabeth presented Fred with a son, but was confined to the High Alps for much of her life. Captain Fred, now Major Fred, and subsequently Colonel Fred, returned to travelling and skirmishing.

Also, to his passion for ballooning. In 1882, he took off from the Dover Gasworks, bound for France. Marooned above the Channel, he thought inevitably of Madame Sarah. He was making the flight he had always promised himself, but now it was not, as she had flirtatiously proposed, towards her. Though he had never spoken to anyone of their liaison, a few suspected it, and occasionally – after a game of cards at Pratt's, followed by a late supper of bacon and eggs and beer – some allusion was nudgingly attempted. But he never rose to the bait. Now, suspended, he heard only her voice in his ear. *Mon cher* Capitaine Fred. It still cut him, after all these years. Impetuously, he lit a cigar. It was a foolish gesture, but at that moment his entire life could explode, for all he cared. His mind drifted back to the rue Fortuny, to her eyes of transparent blue, her hair like a burning bush; to her great cane bed. Then he came to his senses, tossed the half-smoked cigar into the sea, threw out some ballast and sought the higher altitudes, hoping to catch a northerly breeze.

When he landed near the Château de Montigny, the French were as hospitable as he had always found them. They did not even mind his raillery about the superiority of the British political system. They merely fed him some more, and urged him to smoke another cigar in the far safer conditions of their fireside.

On his return to England, he sat down and wrote a book. His flight had taken place on the 23rd of March. *A Ride Across the Channel and Other Adventures In The Air* was published by Samson, Low thirteen days later, on the 5th of April.

On the previous day, the 4th of April 1882, Sarah Bernhardt had married Aristides Damal, a Greek diplomat turned actor, a famously vain and insolent womaniser (also spendthrift, gambler and morphine addict). Since he was Greek Orthodox, and she a Jewish Roman Catholic, the easiest place for them to be married quickly was London: at the Protestant church of St Andrew's, Wells Street. Whether she was able to buy a copy of Fred Burnaby's book to read on her honeymoon is not known. The marriage was a disaster.

Three years later, having illicitly joined Lord Wolseley's expedition to relieve General Gordon at Khartoum, Burnaby was killed at the Battle of Abu Klea by a spear-thrust to the neck from one of the Mahdi's soldiers.

Mrs Burnaby was to marry again; she also established herself as a prolific authoress. Ten years after her first husband's death, she published a manual, now long unavailable, called *Hints on Snow Photography*.

THE LOSS OF DEPTH

You put together two people who have not been put together before. Sometimes it is like that first attempt to harness a hydrogen balloon to a fire balloon: do you prefer crash and burn, or burn and crash? But sometimes it works, and something new is made, and the world is changed. Then, at some point, sooner or later, for this reason or that, one of them is taken away. And what is taken away is greater than the sum of what was there. This may not be mathematically possible; but it is emotionally possible.

After the Battle of Abu Klea there were 'immense hordes of dead Arabs', who were 'by necessity, left unburied'. But not unexamined. Each had a leather band round one arm containing a prayer composed by the Mahdi, who promised his soldiers that it would turn British bullets to water. Love gives us a similar feeling of faith and invincibility. And sometimes, perhaps often, it works. We dodge between bullets as Sarah Bernhardt claimed to dodge between raindrops. But there is always the sudden spear-thrust to the neck. Because every love story is a potential grief story.

✱

Early in life, the world divides crudely into those who have had sex and those who haven't. Later, into those who have known love, and those who haven't. Later still — at least, if we are lucky (or, on the other hand, unlucky) — it divides into those who have endured grief, and those who haven't. These divisions are absolute; they are tropics we cross.

We were together for thirty years. I was thirty-two when we met, sixty-two when she died. The heart of my life; the life of my heart. And though she hated the idea of growing old — in her twenties, she thought she would never live past forty — I happily looked forward to our continuing life together: to things becoming slower and calmer, to collaborative recollection. I could imagine myself taking care of her; I could even — though I didn't — have imagined myself, like Nadar, easing the hair from her aphasiac temples, learning the part of the tender nurse (and the fact that she might have hated such dependency is irrelevant). Instead, from a summer to an autumn, there was anxiety, alarm, fear, terror. It was thirty-seven days from diagnosis to death. I tried never to look away, always to face it; and a kind of crazy lucidity resulted. Most evenings, as I left the hospital, I would find myself staring resentfully at people on buses merely going home at the end of their day. How could they sit there so idly and unknowingly, their indifferent profiles on display, when the world was about to be changed?

We are bad at dealing with death, that banal, unique thing; we can no longer make it part of a wider pattern. And as E. M. Forster put it, 'One death may explain itself, but it throws no light upon another.' So grief in turn becomes unimaginable: not just its length and depth, but its tone and texture, its deceptions and false dawns, its recidivism. Also, its initial shock: you have suddenly come down in the freezing German Ocean, equipped only with an absurd cork overjacket that is supposed to keep you alive.

And you can never prepare for this new reality in which you have been dunked. I know someone who thought, or hoped, she could. Her husband was a long time dying of cancer; being practical, she asked in advance for a reading list, and assembled the classic texts of bereavement. They made no difference when the moment came. 'The moment': that feeling of months which on examination prove only to have been days.

For many years I would occasionally think of an account I read by a woman novelist about the death of her older husband. Amid her grief, she admitted, there was a small inner voice of truth murmuring to her, 'I'm free.' I remembered this when my own time came, fearing that prompter's whisper which would sound like a betrayal. But no such voice was heard, no such words. One grief throws no light upon another.

Grief, like death, is banal and unique. So, a banal comparison. When you change your make of car, you suddenly notice how many other cars of the same sort there are on the road. They register in a way they never did before. When you are widowed, you suddenly notice all the widows and widowers coming towards you. Before, they had been more or less invisible, and they continue to remain so to other drivers, to the unwidowed.

We grieve in character. That too seems obvious, but this is a time when nothing seems or feels obvious. A friend died, leaving a wife and two children. How did they respond? The wife set about redecorating the house; the son went into his father's study and did not emerge until he had read every message, every document, every hint of evidence left behind; the daughter made paper lanterns to float on the lake where her father's ashes were to be cast.

Another friend died, suddenly, catastrophically, by the baggage carousel of a foreign airport. His wife had gone to fetch a trolley; when she returned, there was a scrum of people surrounding something. Perhaps a suitcase had burst open. But no, her husband had burst open, and was already dead. A year or two later, when my wife died, she wrote to me: 'The thing is — nature is so exact, it hurts exactly as much as it is worth, so in a way one relishes the pain, I think. If it didn't matter, it wouldn't matter.' I found this consoling, and kept her letter on my desk for a long time; though I doubted I would ever come to relish the pain. But then I was only at the start of things.

I did already know that only the old words would do: death, grief, sorrow, sadness, heartbreak. Nothing modernly evasive or medicalising. Grief is a human, not a medical, condition, and while there are pills to help us forget it — and everything else — there are no pills to cure it. The griefstruck are not depressed, just properly, appropriately, mathematically ('it hurts exactly as much as it is worth') sad. One euphemistic verb I especially loathed was 'pass'. 'I'm sorry to hear your wife has passed' (as in 'passed water'? 'passed blood'?). You do not have to force the word 'die' on others, even if you always use it yourself. There is a midpoint. At a social event she and I would normally have attended together, an acquaintance came up and said to me, simply, 'There's someone missing.' That felt correct, in both senses.

Griefs do not explain one another, but they may overlap. And so there is a complicity among the griefstruck. Only you know what you know – even if it is just that you know different things. You have stepped through a mirror, as in some Cocteau film, and find yourself in a world reordered in logic and pattern. A small example. Three years before my wife died, an old friend of mine, the poet Christopher Reid, was also widowed. He wrote about his wife's dying and its aftermath. In one poem he described the denial by the living of those who have died:

> but I too have met the tribal will to impose
>   taboos and codes, and have behaved rudely,
> invoking my dead wife in dinner-table conversation.
>   A beat of silence, of shared fear and sick shock, falls.

When I first read these lines, I thought: what strange friends you must have. I also thought: you didn't really believe you were behaving rudely, did you? Later, when my own turn came, I understood. I took the early decision (or, more likely, given the turmoil of my brain, the decision took me) to speak of my wife whenever I wanted or needed to: invoking her would be a normal part of any normal exchange – even though 'normality' was long fled. I swiftly realised how grief sorts out and realigns those around the griefstruck; how friends are tested; how some pass, some fail. Old friendships may deepen through shared sorrow; or suddenly appear lightweight. The young do better than the middle-aged; women better than men. This shouldn't come as a surprise, but it does. After all, you might expect those closest to you in age and sex and marital status to understand best. What a naivety. I remember a 'dinner-table conversation' in a restaurant with three married friends of roughly my age. Each had known her for many years – perhaps eighty or ninety in total – and each would have said, if asked, that they loved her. I mentioned her name; no one picked it up. I did it again, and again nothing. Perhaps the third time I was deliberately trying to provoke, being pissed off at what struck me not as good manners but cowardice. Afraid to touch her name, they denied her thrice, and I thought the worse of them for it.

There is the question of anger. Some are angry with the person who has died, who has abandoned them, betrayed them by losing life. What could be more irrational than that? Few die willingly, not even most suicides. Some of the griefstruck are angry with God, but if He doesn't exist, that too is irrational. Some are angry with the universe for letting it happen, for this being the inevitable, irreversible case. I didn't exactly feel this, but through that autumn of 2008 I read the papers and followed events on television with an overpowering indifference. 'The News' seemed just a larger, more insulting version of those busfuls of unheeding passengers, the fuel of their transport solipsism and ignorance. For some reason I cared a lot about Obama getting elected, but very little about anything else in the world. They said that the whole financial system might be about to crash and burn, but this didn't bother me. Money could not have saved her, so what good was money, and what was the point in saving its neck? They said the world's climate was reaching a point of no return, but it could go to that point and beyond for all it mattered to me. I would drive home from the hospital and at a certain stretch of road, just before a railway bridge, the words would come into my head, and I would repeat them aloud: 'It's just the universe doing its stuff.' That was 'all' that 'it' – this enormous, tremendous 'it' – was. The words didn't hold any consolation; perhaps they were a way of resisting alternative, false consolations. But if the universe was just doing its stuff, it could do its stuff to itself as well, and to hell with it. What did I care about saving the world if the world couldn't, wouldn't, save her?

A friend whose husband died almost instantly of a stroke in his mid-fifties told me of her anger not at him, but at the fact that he *didn't know*. Didn't know he was going to die, didn't have time to prepare, to say farewells to her and their children. This is a form of being angry with the universe. An anger at indifference – the indifference of life merely continuing until it merely ends.

So the anger may be visited instead on friends. For their inability to say or do the right things, for their unwanted pressingness or seeming *froideur*. And since the griefstruck rarely know what they need or want, only what they don't, offence-giving and offence-taking are common. Some friends are as scared of grief as they are of death; they avoid you as if they fear infection. Some, without knowing it, half expect you to do their mourning for them. Others put on a bright practicality. 'So,' a voice on the phone asks, a week after I have buried my wife, 'what are you up to? Are you going on walking holidays?' I shout at the phone for a moment or two, then put it down. No: walking holidays were what we did together, when my life was on the level.

But strangely, in retrospect, this impertinent question wasn't too far out. I had occasionally, over the years, imagined what I might do if 'something bad' happened in my life. I did not specify the 'something bad' to myself, but the possibilities were very limited. I decided in advance that I would do one trivial and one more serious thing. The first was that I would finally succumb to Rupert Murdoch and sign up for a panoply of sports channels. The second would be to walk, by myself, across France – or, if that seemed unfeasible, across a corner of it, specifically along the Canal du Midi, from the Mediterranean to the Atlantic, my rucksack containing a notebook in which I would record my attempts to deal with the 'something bad'. But when it happened, I had no desire to pull on my boots. And 'walking holiday' would hardly be the name for such a grief-trudge.

Other distractions were proposed, other advice given. Some reacted as if the death of the loved one were merely an extreme form of divorce. I was advised to get a dog. I would reply sarcastically that this did not seem much of a substitute for a wife. I was warned by a widow to 'try not to notice other couples' – but most of my friends form couples. Someone suggested I rent a flat in Paris for six months, or, failing that, 'a beach cabin in Guadeloupe'. She and her husband would look after my house while I was away. This would be convenient for them, and 'we'd have a garden for Freddie'. The proposal came by email during the last day of my wife's life. And Freddie was their dog.

Of course, the Silent Ones and the advice givers will be feeling grief of their own, and perhaps their own anger, which may be aimed at us – at me. They might be wanting to say: 'Your grief is an embarrassment. We're just waiting for it to pass. And, by the way, you're less interesting without her.' (This is true: I do feel less interesting without her. When, alone, I talk to her, I am worth listening to; when I talk to myself, not. 'Oh, stop boring me,' I say in voiced rebuke, as I repeat myself to myself.) Yes, if they thought that, I'd agree. An American friend told me straightforwardly, 'I always thought she'd see you out.' I quite understood: my survival had seemed the less likely possibility. But perhaps he also meant that he would have preferred her survival to mine. And I could hardly quarrel with that either.

Nor do you know how you appear to others. How you feel and how you look may or may not be the same. So how do you feel? As if you have dropped from a height of several hundred feet, conscious all the time, have landed feet first in a rose bed with an impact that has driven you in up to the knees, and whose shock has caused your internal organs to rupture and burst forth from your body. That is what it feels like, and why should it look any different? No wonder some want to swerve away to a safer topic of conversation. And perhaps they are not avoiding death, and her; they are avoiding you.

I do not believe I shall ever see her again. Never see, hear, touch, embrace, listen to, laugh with; never again wait for her footstep, smile at the sound of an opening door, fit her body into mine, mine into hers. Nor do I believe we shall meet again in some dematerialised form. I believe dead is dead. Some think grief a kind of violent if justifiable self-pity; some that it is merely one's own reflection in death's eye; others say it's the survivor they feel sorry for, because they're the one going through it, whereas the lost loved one can no longer suffer. Such approaches try to handle grief by minimising it – and doing the same with death. It's true that some of my grief is self-directed – look what I have lost, look how my life has been diminished – but it is more, much more, and has been from the beginning, about her: look what *she* has lost, now that she has lost life. Her body, her spirit; her radiant curiosity about life. At times it feels as if life itself is the greatest loser, the true bereaved party, because it is no longer subjected to that radiant curiosity of hers.

The griefstruck are angered when others shy away from the facts, the truth, even the simple use of a name. Yet how much truth do the griefstruck themselves tell, and how often do they collude in evasion? Because the truths they have fallen into, not just up to their knees, but their hearts, necks, brains, are sometimes indefinable; or even if definable, inexpressible. I remember a friend who suffered from gallstones and had an operation for their removal. He said it had been the most painful thing he had ever endured. He was a journalist, and used to describing things; I asked if he could describe the pain. He looked at me, his eyes watered at the memory, and he remained silent; he couldn't find words which came close to being useful. And words fail also at a lower, merely conversational level. When I was hot in grief an acquaintance asked me, in front of others, 'So, how are you?' I shook my head to imply that this wasn't the place (it was across a noisy lunch table). He persisted, as if helpfully refining the question, 'No, but how are you in yourself?' I waved him away; besides, I felt not *in* myself but way out of myself. I could have passed it off by saying, for example, 'A bit up and down.' That would have been a proper, prim and English answer. Except that the griefstruck rarely feel either proper, prim, or even English.

You ask yourself: to what extent in this turmoil of missing am I missing her, or missing the life we had together, or missing what it was in her that made me more myself, or missing simple companionship, or (not so simple) love, or all or any overlapping bits of each? You ask yourself: what happiness is there in just the memory of happiness? And how in any case might that work, given that happiness has only ever consisted of something shared? Solitary happiness — it sounds like a contradiction in terms, an implausible contraption that will never get off the ground.

The question of suicide arrives early, and quite logically. Most days I pass the stretch of pavement I was looking across at when the idea first came to me. I will give it x months, or x years (up to a maximum of two), and then, if I cannot live without her, if my life is reduced to mere passive continuance, I shall become active. I knew soon enough my preferred method — a hot bath, a glass of wine next to the taps, and an exceptionally sharp Japanese carving knife. I thought of that solution fairly often, and still do. They say (there is a lot of 'they say' around grief and grief-bearing) that thinking about suicide reduces the risk of suicide. I don't know if this is true: for some, it must help them elaborate their planning. So, presumably, thinking about it can cut both ways.

A friend whose partner died of Aids after they had been together eight years said two things to me: 'It's just a question of getting through the night' and 'There's only one good thing — you can do what you like.' The first was not a problem for me — you just get the right pills in the right dosage; no, the problem was rather getting through the *day*. As for doing what I liked: for me, this usually meant doing things with her. Insofar as I liked doing things by myself, it was partly for the pleasure of telling her about them afterwards. Besides, what did I now want to do? I didn't want to walk the length of the Canal du Midi. I wanted, very strongly and exactly, the opposite: to stay at home, in the spaces she had created and where she still, in my imagination, moved. As for pigging out on any and every major purchasable sporting fixture, I found that my needs were very particular. In those first months, I wanted to watch sport in which I had almost no emotional involvement at all. I would enjoy — though that verb is too strong to describe a kind of listless attending — football matches between, say, Middlesbrough and Slovan Bratislava (ideally the second leg of a tie whose first leg I had missed), in some low-level European tournament which mostly excited those in Middlesbrough and Bratislava. I wanted to watch sport to which I would normally be indifferent. Because now I could only be indifferent; I had no emotions left to lend.

I mourn her uncomplicatedly, and absolutely. This is my good luck, and also my bad luck. Early on, the words came into my head: I miss her in every action, and in every inaction. It was one of those phrases I repeated to myself as confirmation of where and what I was. Just as, driving home, I would prepare myself for my return by saying out loud: 'I am going back neither with her nor to her.' Just as, when something failed, was broken or mislaid, I would reassure myself with: 'On the scale of loss, it is nothing.' But such is the solipsism of grief that I barely thought about gradations and differences until a woman friend said that she envied me my grief. Why on earth, I asked. Because 'If X [her husband] died, it would be more complicated for me.' She did not elaborate; nor did she need to. And I thought: maybe, in a way, I'm having it easy.

The first time I was ever away from her for more than a day or two – I had gone down to the country to write – I discovered that, on top of (or, perhaps, beneath) all the predictable ways, I also missed her morally. This came as a surprise, but maybe it shouldn't have. Love may not lead where we think or hope, but regardless of outcome it should be a call to seriousness and truth. If it is not that – if it is not moral in its effect – then love is no more than an exaggerated form of pleasure. Whereas grief, love's opposite, does not seem to occupy a moral space. The defensive, curled position it forces us into if we are to survive makes us more selfish. It is not a place of upper air; there are no views. You can no longer hear yourself living.

✳

Before, when I read newspaper obituaries, I used to idly calculate my age against the dead person's: x more years, I would think (or, already, x fewer). Now I read obituaries and check how long the subject was married. I envy those who had more time than I did. It rarely crosses my mind that they might have been living, with every extra year, some terrible extra boredom or servitude. I am not interested in that sort of marriage; I want to award them only happy years. But then I also calculate the length of widowhoods. Here, for instance, is Eugene Polley, 1915–2012, the inventor of the TV remote control. At the end of his obituary it says: 'Polley's wife, Blanche, to whom he was married for 34 years, died in 1976.' And I think: married for longer than me, and still widowed for thirty-six years. Three and a half decades of relishing the pain?

Someone I had only met twice wrote to tell me that a few months previously he had 'lost his wife to cancer' (another phrase that jarred: compare 'We lost our dog to gypsies', or 'He lost his wife to a commercial traveller'). He reassured me that one does survive the grief; moreover, one emerges a 'stronger', and in some ways a 'better', person. This struck me as outrageous and self-praising (as well as too quickly decided). How could I possibly be a better person without her than with her? Later, I thought: but he is just echoing Nietzsche's line about what doesn't kill us making us stronger. And as it happens, I have long considered this epigram particularly specious. There are many things that fail to kill us but weaken us for ever. Ask anyone who deals with victims of torture. Ask rape counsellors and those who handle domestic violence. Look around at those emotionally damaged by mere ordinary life.

Grief reconfigures time, its length, its texture, its function: one day means no more than the next, so why have they been picked out and given separate names? It also reconfigures space. You have entered a new geography, mapped by a new cartography. You seem to be taking your bearings from one of those seventeenth-century maps which feature the Desert of Loss, the (windless) Lake of Indifference, the (dried-up) River of Desolation, the Bog of Self-Pity, and the (subterranean) Caverns of Memory.

In this new-found-land there is no hierarchy, except that of feeling, of pain. Who has fallen from the greater height, who has spilt more organs on the ground? Except that it rarely seems as straightforward – straightforwardly sad – as this. There is a grotesquerie to grief as well. You lose the sense of your existence being rational, or justifiable. You feel absurd, like one of those dressed mannequins, surrounded by skulls, that Nadar photographed in the Catacombs. Or like that boa constrictor which took to swallowing sofa cushions and had to be shot dead.

I look at my key ring (which used to be hers): it holds only two keys, one to the front door of the house and one to the back gate of the cemetery. This is my life, I think. I notice strange continuities: I used to rub oil into her back because her skin dried easily; now I rub oil into the drying oak of her grave-marker. But what seems to have disappeared is a feel for the pattern of things. At the start of his life, Fred Burnaby jumped twenty feet off a piece of gymnastic equipment and broke his leg. Towards the end of her life, while playing La Tosca, Sarah Bernhardt jumped off the battlements of Castel Sant'Angelo only to discover that the stagehands had forgotten to pile up mattresses to cushion her fall; she broke her leg. For that matter, Nadar broke his leg when *The Giant* crashed; and my wife broke her leg on our front steps. This might as well be a pattern, you think, whereas before it would have seemed a strange but trivial coincidence, just a question of height, of how far each of us falls in life. Perhaps grief, which destroys all patterns, destroys even more: the belief that any pattern exists. But we cannot, I think, survive without such belief. So each of us must pretend to find, or re-erect, a pattern. Writers believe in the patterns their words make, which they hope and trust add up to ideas, to stories, to truths. This is always their salvation, whether griefless or griefstruck.

First Nietzsche, then Nadar. God is dead, and no longer there to see us. So *we* must see us. And Nadar gave us the distance, the height, to do so. He gave us God's distance, the God's-eye view. And where it ended (for the moment) was with Earthrise and those photographs taken from lunar orbit, in which our planet looks more or less like any other planet (except to an astronomer): silent, revolving, beautiful, dead, irrelevant. Which may have been how God saw us, and why He absented himself. Of course I don't believe in the Absenting God, but such a story makes a nice pattern.

When we killed – or exiled – God, we also killed ourselves. Did we notice that sufficiently at the time? No God, no afterlife, no us. We were right to kill Him, of course, this long-standing imaginary friend of ours. And we weren't going to get an afterlife anyway. But we sawed off the branch we were sitting on. And the view from there, from that height – even if it was only the illusion of a view – wasn't so bad.

We have lost God's height, and gained Nadar's; but we have also lost depth. Once, a long time ago, we could go down into the Underworld, where the dead still lived. Now, that metaphor is lost to us, and we can only go down literally: potholing, drilling for minerals, and so on. Instead of the Underworld, the Underground. Some of us will go down into the earth at the end of it all. Not very far, just six feet down; except that the scale of depth is lost as you stand there and throw flowers down on to a coffin lid, whose brass nameplate winks back at you. Then, it looks and feels a long way down, six feet.

Some people, as if to avoid such depth and regain a little height, have their ashes sent up into the sky in a rocket: as close to heaven as we can get. Sarah Bernhardt and her companions cheerfully loosed ballast on to the upturned faces of astonished groundlings – English tourists, a French wedding party. Perhaps someone, looking up at a sudden rocket in the sky, has already received a faceful of human ash not long from the crematorium. In the future, no doubt, the rich and famous will send their ashes up into Earth orbit, even Moon orbit.

There is the question of grief versus mourning. You can try to differentiate them by saying that grief is a state while mourning is a process; yet they inevitably overlap. Is the state diminishing? Is the process progressing? How to tell? Perhaps it's easier to think of them metaphorically. Grief is vertical — and vertiginous — while mourning is horizontal. Grief makes your stomach turn, snatches the breath from you, cuts off the blood supply to the brain; mourning blows you in a new direction. But since you are now in enveloping cloud, it is impossible to tell if you are marooned or deceptively in motion. You do not have some useful little invention consisting of a tiny paper parachute attached to fifty yards of silk line. All you know is that you have small power to affect things. You are a first-time aeronaut, alone beneath the gasbag, equipped with a few kilos of ballast, and told that this item in your hand you've never seen before is the valve-line.

Initially, you continue doing what you used to do with her, out of familiarity, love, the need for a pattern. Soon, you realise the trap you are in: caught between repeating what you did with her, but without her, and so missing her; or doing new things, things you never did with her, and so missing her differently. You feel sharply the loss of shared vocabulary, of tropes, teases, short cuts, injokes, sillinesses, faux rebukes, amatory footnotes — all those obscure references rich in memory but valueless if explained to an outsider.

All couples, even the most bohemian, build up patterns

in their lives together, and these patterns have an annual cycle. So Year One is like a negative image of the year you have been used to. Instead of being studded with events, it is now studded with non-events: Christmas, your birthday, her birthday, anniversary of the day you met, wedding anniversary. And these are overlaid with new anniversaries: of the day fear arrived, the day she first fell, the day she went into hospital, the day she came out of hospital, the day she died, the day she was buried.

You think that Year Two can't be worse than Year One, and imagine yourself prepared for it. You think you have met all the different sorts of pain you will be asked to bear, and that after this there will only be repetition. But why should repetition mean less pain? Those first repetitions invite you to contemplate all the repetitions to come in future years. Grief is the negative image of love; and if there can be accumulation of love over the years, then why not of grief?

And there are still new, one-off pains for which you are quite unprepared, and unprotected against. Like sitting round a table with your seven-year-old great-niece while she amuses the company with her new game of Odd Man Out. So-and-so is the odd man/woman out because of blue eyes/brown jacket/goldfish ownership, and so on. Then, from nowhere, except from childlike logic: 'Julian's the odd one out because he's the only person whose wife is dead.'

It took a while, but I remember the moment – or rather, the suddenly arriving argument – which made it less likely that I would kill myself. I realised that, insofar as she was alive at all, she was alive in my memory. Of course, she remained powerfully in other people's minds as well; but I was her principal rememberer. If she was anywhere, she was within me, internalised. This was normal. And it was equally normal – and irrefutable – that I could not kill myself because then I would also be killing her. She would die a second time, my lustrous memories of her fading as the bathwater turned red. So it was, in the end (or, at least, for the time being), simply decided. As was the broader, but related question: how am I to live? I must live as she would have wanted me to.

After a few months, I began to brave public places and go out to a play, a concert, an opera. But I found that I had developed a terror of the foyer. Not of the space itself, but of what it contained: cheerful, expectant, normal people looking forward to enjoying themselves. I couldn't bear the noise and the look of placid normality: just more busloads of people indifferent to my wife's dying. Friends were obliged to meet me outside the theatre and conduct me, like a child, to my seat. Once there, I felt safe; and when the lights went down, safer.

The first play I was taken to was *Oedipus*; the first opera, Strauss's *Elektra*. But as I sat through these harshest of tragedies, in which the gods inflict intolerable punishment for human offence, I didn't feel myself transported to a distant, antique culture where terror and pity reigned. I felt instead that *Oedipus* and *Elektra* were coming to me, to my land, to the new geography I now inhabited. And, quite unexpectedly, I fell into a love of opera. For most of my life it had seemed one of the least comprehensible art forms. I didn't really understand what was going on (despite the diligent reading of plot summaries); I was prejudiced against those dinner-jacketed picnickers who seemed to own the genre; but most of all, I couldn't make the necessary imaginative leap. Operas felt like deeply implausible and badly constructed plays, with characters yelling in one another's faces simultaneously. The initial problem – that of comprehension – was fixed by the introduction of surtitles. But now, in the darkness of an auditorium and the darkness of grief, the form's implausibility suddenly dissolved. Now it seemed quite natural for people to stand onstage and sing at one another, because song was a more primal means of communication than the spoken word – both higher and deeper. In Verdi's *Don Carlo* the hero has scarcely met his French princess in the Forest of Fontainebleau before he is on his knees singing, 'My name is Carlo and I love you.' *Yes*, I thought, that's right, that's how life is and should be, let's concentrate on the essentials. Of course, opera has plot – and I was already anticipating all those unknown stories I was about to discover – but its main function is to deliver the characters as swiftly as possible to the point where they can sing of their deepest emotions. Opera cuts to the chase – as death does. So now, contented indifference before Middlesbrough against Slovan Bratislava coexisted with a craving for an art in which violent, overwhelming, hysterical and destructive emotion was the norm; an art which seeks, more obviously than any other form, to break your heart. Here was my new social realism.

I went to a London cinema for a direct broadcast from New York of Gluck's *Orfeo ed Euridice*. Beforehand, I did my homework, listening through to the piece, libretto in hand. And I thought: this can't possibly work. A man's wife dies, and his lamentation so moves the gods that they grant him permission to go down into the Underworld, find her, and bring her back. One condition, however, is applied: he must not look her in the face until they are back on earth, or she will be lost to him for ever. Whereupon, as he is leading her out of the Underworld, she persuades him to look back at her; whereupon she dies; whereupon he laments her again, even more affectingly, and draws his sword to commit suicide; whereupon the God of Love, disarmed by this display of uxoriousness, restores Euridice to life. Oh, come off it, *really*. It wasn't the presence or the actions of the gods – those I could easily credit; it was the fact that no one in his senses would turn and look at Euridice, knowing what the consequence would be. And if that wasn't enough, the role of Orfeo, originally a castrato or countertenor but nowadays a trouser role, was to be taken in this production by a bulky contralto. Yet I had quite underestimated *Orfeo*, the opera most immaculately targeted at the griefstruck; and in that cinema the miraculous trickery of art happened again. *Of course* Orfeo would turn to look at the pleading Euridice – how could he not? Because, while 'no one in his senses' would do so, he is quite out of his senses with love and grief and hope. You lose the world for a glance? Of course you do. That is what the world is for: to lose under the right circumstances. How could *anyone* hold to their vow with Euridice's voice at their back?

The gods impose terms and conditions on Orfeo when he goes down into the Underworld; he must agree to the deal.

Death often brings out the bargainer in us. How many times have you read in books, or seen in films, or heard in the general narrative of life, about someone promising God – or whoever might be Up There – to behave in such-and-such a way if only He will spare them, or the one they love, or both of them? When it came to my turn – in those dread-filled thirty-seven days – I was never tempted to bargain because there was and is no one in my cosmos to bargain with. Would I give all my books for her life? Would I give my own life for hers? Facile to say yes: such questions were rhetorical, hypothetical, operatic. 'Why?' the child asks, '*why?*' The unyielding parent answers simply, 'Because.' So, as I drove towards that railway bridge, I would doggedly repeat, 'It's just the universe doing its stuff.' I said it to avoid being led astray by vain hopes and meaningless diversions.

I told one of the few Christians I know that she was seriously ill. He replied that he would pray for her. I didn't object, but shockingly soon found myself informing him, not without bitterness, that his god didn't seem to have been very effective. He replied, 'Have you ever considered that she might have suffered more?' Ah, I thought, so that's the best your pale Galilean and his dad can do.

And that bridge I passed under was in the meantime coming to represent more than just a bridge. It had been built to carry the Eurostar into its new London terminus at St Pancras. The switch from Waterloo was more convenient, and I had often imagined us going on it together, to Paris, Brussels and beyond. But somehow, we never did, and now never would. And so this unoffending bridge came to stand for part of our lost future, for all the spurts and segments and divagations of life that we would now never share; but also for things undone in the past – for promises unkept, for carelessness and unkindness, times of falling short. I came to hate and fear that bridge, though never changed my route.

A year or so later, I saw *Orfeo* again, this time live, and in modern dress. The production began, atypically, by staging the death of Euridice. There is a cocktail party; all are having fun; we deduce that she is the cynosure in the red frock. Suddenly, she collapses to the floor. The guests surround her, Orfeo kneels to attend her, but she is losing height, fatally, falling slowly through a trapdoor in the boards. He clutches at her, trying to hold her back, but she slips away, out of his fingers and out of her frock, so that he is left on stage grasping just a swathe of emptied cloth.

In modern dress, the opera still worked its magic trick. And yet, in modern dress ourselves, we cannot be Orfeo, or Euridice. We have lost the old metaphors, and must find new ones. We can't go down as he went down. So we must go down in a different way, bring her back in a different way. We can still go down in dreams. And we can go down in memory.

At first, improbably (but then where has probability gone in all of this?), dreams are more reliable, more secure, than memory. In dreams she arrives looking and acting very like herself. I always know it is her – she is calm, and amused, and happy, and sexy, and so, as a result, am I. The dream falls swiftly and regularly into a pattern. We are together, she is clearly in good health, so I think – or rather, since this is a dream, I know – that either she has been misdiagnosed, or she has made a miraculous recovery, or (at the very least) that death has somehow been postponed for several years and our life together can continue. This illusion lasts for a while. But then I think – or rather, since this is a dream, I know – that I must be inside a dream because, actually, she is dead. I wake happy at having had the illusion, yet dismayed at how truth has ended it; so I never try to re-enter that dream again.

Some nights, after turning out the light, I remind her

that she hasn't been in my dreams recently, and often she responds by coming to me (or rather, 'she' 'responds' by coming – I never think for a moment that all this is other than self-generated). Sometimes in these dreams we kiss; always there is a kind of laughing lightness to the scenario. She never reproaches or rebukes me, or makes me feel guilty or neglectful (though since I regard these dreams as self-generated, then I must also regard them as self-serving, even self-satisfied). Perhaps the dreams are as they are because there is enough regret and self-reproach in real, lived time. But they are always a source of comfort.

The more so because when I seek to go down in memory, I fail. For a long time I cannot remember back before the start of the year in which she died. All I can do is January to October: three weeks in Chile and Argentina, with my sixty-second birthday spent in a high forest of monkey-puzzle trees, full of cavorting Magellanic woodpeckers. Then normal life again, before a walking holiday in Sicily, and some of our last joint memories: giant fennel and a hillside of wild flowers, an Antonello da Messina and a stuffed porcupine, a fishing town filled with the putt-putt celebrants of World Vespa Weekend. But then, on our return, apprehension, rising fear, the sudden crash. I remember every detail of her decline, her time in hospital, return home, dying, burial.

But I cannot get back beyond that January; my memory seems burnt away. A widowed colleague of hers assures me that this is not unusual, that my memories will return, but there are few certainties left in my life, and nothing follows a pattern, so I am sceptical. Why should anything happen when everything has happened? And so it feels as if she is slipping away from me a second time: first I lose her in the present, then I lose her in the past. Memory — the mind's photographic archive — is failing.

And this is where the Silent Ones cause further offence. They do not understand (how could they?) that they have a new function in your life. You need your friends not just as friends, but also as corroborators. The chief witness to what has been your life is now silenced, and retrospective doubt is inevitable. So you need them to tell you, however glancingly, however unintendingly, that what you once were — the two of you — was seen. Not just known from within but seen from without: witnessed, corroborated, and remembered with an accuracy of which you are yourself currently incapable.

Though I remember, sharply, last things. The last book she read. The last play (and film, and concert, and opera, and art exhibition) that we went to together. The last wine she drank, the last clothes she bought. The last weekend away.

The last bed we slept in that wasn't ours. The last this, the last that. The last piece of my writing that made her laugh. The last words she wrote herself; the last time she signed her name. The last piece of music I played her when she came home. Her last complete sentence. Her last spoken word.

In 1960, an American friend of ours, then a young writer in London, found herself, after lunch at the Travellers' Club, sharing a taxi home with Ivy Compton-Burnett. At first Compton-Burnett talked to our friend, in a normal conversational tone, about the club, their host, the food, and so on. Then, with a marginal shift of the head, but absolutely no shift of tone, she started talking to Margaret Jourdain, her companion of thirty years. The fact that Jourdain, far from being in the cab with them, had been dead since 1951 made no difference. That was who she wanted to talk to, and did so for the rest of the journey back to South Kensington.

This strikes me as quite normal. We are not surprised when children have imaginary friends. Why be surprised when adults have them too? Except that these friends are real as well.

Bonnard used to paint his model/mistress/wife Marthe as a young woman naked in the bath. He painted her like this when she was no longer young. He continued to paint her like this after she was dead. An art critic, reviewing a Bonnard show in London some ten or fifteen years ago, called this 'morbid'. Even at the time it struck me as the opposite, and entirely normal.

Ivy Compton-Burnett missed Margaret Jourdain with 'palpable, angry vehemence'. To one friend she wrote, 'I wish you had met her, and so met more of me.' After being made a Dame of the British Empire, she wrote: 'The one I miss most, Margaret Jourdain, has now been dead sixteen years, and I still have to tell her things . . . I am not fully a Dame, as she does not know about it.' This is true, and defines the lostness of the griefstruck. You constantly report things, so that the loved one 'knows'. You may be aware that you are fooling yourself (though, if aware, are at the same time not fooling yourself), yet you continue. And everything you do, or might achieve thereafter, is thinner, weaker, matters less. There is no echo coming back; no texture, no resonance, no depth of field.

As a former lexicographer, I am a descriptivist rather than a prescriptivist. English always has been in a state of flux; there was no golden age when words and meanings matched, and the language stood firm and grand like mortarless walls: words are born, live, decay and die — it's just the linguistic universe doing its stuff. However, as a writer, and as a normally prejudiced English-speaking citizen, I can growl and moan with the best of them: for example, when people think 'decimate' means 'massacre', or weaken the usefully separate meaning of 'disinterested'. Nowadays, as with 'to pass' and 'losing one's wife to cancer', I bridle at the misuse of the adjective 'uxorious'. If we don't look out, it will come to describe 'a man who has many wives', or even (that dubious phrase) 'a lover of women'. It doesn't mean this. It describes – and always will, whatever future dictionaries may permit – a man who loves his wife. A man like Odilon Redon, who for thirty years adored and painted his wife, Camille Falte. In 1869, he wrote:

> You can tell the nature of a man from his companion or his wife. Every woman explains the man by whom she is loved, and vice versa: he explains her character. It is rare for an observer not to find between them a host of intimate and delicate connections. I believe that the greatest happiness will always result from the greatest harmony.

He wrote this not as a complacent husband, but as a solitary observer, nine years before he even met Camille. They married in 1880. Eighteen years later, looking back, he reflected:

I am convinced that the *Yes* I uttered on our wedding day was an expression of the most complete and the most unambiguous certainty that I have ever felt. A certainty more absolute than any I have felt about my vocation.

Ford Madox Ford said, 'You marry to continue the conversation.' Why allow death to interrupt it? The critic H. L. Mencken was married to his wife Sara for a period of four years and nine months. Then she died. Five years into widowerhood, he wrote:

> It is a literal fact that I still think of Sara every day of my life and almost every hour of the day. Whenever I see anything she would have liked I find myself saying I'll buy it and take it to her, and I am always thinking of things to tell her.

This is what those who haven't crossed the tropic of grief often fail to understand: the fact that someone is dead may mean that they are not alive, but doesn't mean that they do not exist.

So I talk to her constantly. This feels as normal as it is necessary. I comment on what I am doing (or have done in the course of the day); I point out things to her while driving; I articulate her responses. I keep alive our lost private language. I tease her and she teases me back; we know the lines by heart. Her voice calms me and gives me courage. I look across at a small photograph on my desk in which she wears a slightly quizzical expression, and answer her quizzing, whatever it might be about. Banal domestic issues are lightened by a brief discussion: she confirms that the bath mat is a disgrace and should be thrown away. Outsiders might find this an eccentric, or 'morbid', or self-deceiving, habit; but outsiders are by definition those who have not known grief. I externalise her easily and naturally because by now I have internalised her. The paradox of grief: if I have survived what is now four years of her absence, it is because I have had four years of her presence. And her active continuance disproves what I earlier pessimistically asserted. Grief can, after all, in some ways, turn out to be a moral space.

Though she always answers when I talk to her, there are limits to my ventriloquism. I can remember – or imagine – what she will say about something that has happened before, or is being closely repeated. But I cannot voice her reaction to new events. Near the start of Year Five, the son of close friends, a gentle, brilliant boy, who grew into a gentle, troubled man, killed himself. Though grounded in grief, I found myself bewildered, unable for several days to react fully to this terrible death. Then I understood why: because I was unable to talk to her, hear her replies, revive and compare our shared memories. Among all the other categories of companion I had lost in her, here was another: my co-griever.

A friend gave me Antonio Tabucchi's *Pereira Maintains*, a novel set in Lisbon in 1938 and much concerned with death and memory. Its main character is an uxorious journalist whose wife has died some years before of consumption. Pereira, now overweight and unhealthy, checks into a thalassotherapy clinic run by Dr Crodoso, the brusque and secular 'wise man' of the story, who advises his patient that he must slough off the past and learn to live in the present. 'If you go on this way,' Crodoso warns, 'you'll end up talking to your wife's photograph.' Pereira replies that he always has, and still does: 'I tell it everything that happens to me and it's as if the picture answered me.' Crodoso is dismissive: 'These are fantasies dictated by the superego.' Pereira's problem, the over-certain doctor insists, is that he 'has not yet done his grief-work'.

Grief-work. It sounds such a clear and solid concept, with its confident two-part name. But it is fluid, slippery, metamorphic. Sometimes it is passive, a waiting for time and pain to disappear; sometimes active, a conscious attention to death and loss and the loved one; sometimes necessarily distractive (the bland football match, the overwhelming opera). And you have never done this kind of work before. It is unpaid, and yet not voluntary; it is rigorous, yet there is no overseer; it is skilled, yet there is no apprenticeship. And it is hard to tell whether you are making progress; or what would help you do so. Theme song for youth (sung by the Supremes): 'You Can't Hurry Love'. Theme song for age (arranged for any instrument): 'You Can't Hurry Grief'.

The more so because, among its repetitions, it is always looking for new ways to prick you. For many years we had a Congolese postman, Jean-Pierre, to whom I would often chat. A year or two before she died, he was switched to a new delivery route. I ran into him again at some point in Year Three. We exchanged politenesses, and then he asked, *'Et comment va Madame?'* *'Madame est morte,'* I found myself saying, and as I explained, and dealt with his shock, I was thinking, even as I was speaking: now I'm having to do it all again *in French*. A completely new pain. And such moments of being sideswiped continue. Towards the end of Year Four, I was coming home in a taxi late one evening, some time after eleven. I always miss her on such occasions –

no companionable debriefing, no silent sleepy presence, no hand in mine. As we neared home, the cabbie began chatting. All was pleasant, and banal, until the cheerful enquiry, 'Your wife, be asleep, will she?' After a silent choke, I gave the only reply I could find. 'I hope so.'

Not everyone values uxoriousness, of course. Some view it as timidity, others as possessiveness. And for the Ancients, Orpheus was far from the exemplar we have turned him into. They thought that if he missed his wife so much, he should have hurried up and joined her in the Underworld by the quick, conventional method of suicide. Plato dismissed him as a wimpy minstrel too cowardly to die for the sake of love: rightly did the gods have him torn to pieces by the maenads.

You need to establish where you are and how lies the ground beneath; but surveying from a balloon never did prove possible. Others helpfully – and hopefully – log your position for you. 'Oh,' they say, 'you're looking better.' Even, 'Much better.' The language of illness, inevitably; and the diagnosis is simple – always the same. But the prognosis? You are not ill in any normal manner. At best you have one of those debilitating conditions which come in many forms, and which some people decline to admit actually exist. 'Throw off your grief,' such doubters imply, 'and we can all go back to pretending that death doesn't exist, or at least is comfortably far away.' A journalist friend was once found weeping at her desk by her section editor. She explained what was already known – that her father had died six weeks previously. The editor replied, 'I thought you'd be over it by now.'

When might you expect to be 'over it'? The griefstruck themselves can hardly tell, since time is now so less measurable than it used to be. Four years on, some say to me, 'You look happier' – making the advance on 'better'. The bolder then add, 'Have you found someone?' As if that were obviously and necessarily the solution. For some outsiders it is; for others not. Some kindly want to 'solve' you; others remain attached to that couple which no longer exists, and for them 'finding someone' would be almost offensive. 'It would be like your dad getting married again,' said a younger friend of mine. By contrast, a long-time American friend of my wife's told me, within weeks of her death, that, statistically, those who have been happy in marriage remarry much sooner than those who have not: often within six months. She meant it encouragingly, but this fact, if it was one (perhaps it only applies in the States, where emotional optimism is a constitutional duty), shocked me. It seemed at the same time perfectly logical and perfectly illogical.

The same friend, four years later, said, 'I resent the fact that she's become part of the past.' If this isn't yet true for me, the grammar, like everything else, has begun to shift: she exists not really in the present, not wholly in the past, but in some intermediate tense, the past-present. Perhaps this is why I relish hearing even the slightest new thing about her: a previously unreported memory, a piece of advice she gave years ago, a flashback of her in ordinary animation. I take surrogate pleasure in her appearances in other people's dreams — how she behaves and is dressed, what she eats, how close she is now to how she was then; also, whether I am there with her. Such fugitive moments excite me, because they briefly re-anchor her in the present, rescue her from the past-present, and delay a little longer that inevitable slippage into the past historic.

Dr Johnson well understood the 'tormenting and harassing want' of grief; and he warned against isolationism and withdrawal. 'An attempt to preserve life in a state of neutrality and indifference is unreasonable and vain. If by excluding joy we could shut out grief, the scheme would deserve very serious attention.' But it doesn't. Nor do extreme measures, like the attempt to 'drag [the heart] by force into scenes of merriment'; or its opposite, the attempt 'to soothe it into tranquillity by making it acquainted with miseries more dreadful and afflictive'. For Johnson, only work and time mitigate grief. 'Sorrow is a kind of rust of the soul, which every new idea contributes in its passage to scour away.'

Grief-workers are self-employed. I wonder if those who are actually self-employed do better at it than those who go to an office or a factory. Perhaps there are statistics for this too. But I think that grief is the place where statistics run out. 'What instruments we have agree,' wrote Auden on the death of Yeats, 'the day of his death was a cold dark day.' Instruments can tell us this much on the day itself. But afterwards, beyond? The needle goes off the dial; the thermometer fails to register; barometers burst. Life's sonar is broken and you can no longer tell how far below the seabed lies.

We go down in dreams, and we go down in memory. And yes, it is true, the memory of earlier times does return, but in the meanwhile we have been made fearful, and I am not sure it is the same memory that returns. How could it be, because it can no longer be corroborated by the one who was there at the time. What we did, where we went, whom we met, how we felt. How we were together. All that. 'We' are now watered down to 'I'. Binocular memory has become monocular. There is no longer the possibility of assembling from two uncertain memories of the same event a surer, single one, by triangulation, by aerial surveying. And so that memory, now in the first person-singular, changes. Less the memory of an event than the memory of a photograph of the event. And nowadays – having lost height, precision, focus – we are no longer sure we trust photography as we once did. Those old familiar snaps of happier times have come to seem less primal, less like photographs of life itself, more like photographs of photographs.

Or, to put it another way, your memory of your life – your previous life – resembles that ordinary miracle witnessed by Fred Burnaby, Captain Colvile and Mr Lucy somewhere near the Thames estuary. They were above the cloud, beneath the sun, and Burnaby had just been emboldened to take off his coat and sit complacently in his shirtsleeves. One of the three saw the phenomenon first and drew it to the attention of the others. The sun was projecting on to the bank of fleecy cloud below the image of their craft: the gasbag, the cradle and, clearly outlined, silhouettes of the three aeronauts. Burnaby compared it to a 'colossal photograph'. And so it is with our life: so clear, so sure, until, for one reason or another – the balloon moves, the cloud disperses, the sun changes angle – the image is lost for ever, available only to memory, turned into anecdote.

✳

There is a man in Venice I remember as clearly as if I had photographed him; or, perhaps, more clearly because I didn't. It was some years ago, one late autumn or early winter. She and I were wandering in an untouristy part of the city, and she had gone ahead of me. I was starting to cross a small, banal bridge when I saw a man coming towards me. He was probably in his sixties, and dressed very correctly. I remember a smart black overcoat, black scarf, black shoes, perhaps a small moustache, and probably a hat – a black homburg. He might have been a Venetian *avvocato*, and he certainly wasn't giving tourists a glance. But I gave him one, because at the bridge's low zenith he took out a white handkerchief and wiped his eyes: not idly, not practically – it wasn't, I'm sure, the cold – but in a slow, concentrated, familiar fashion. I found myself then, and later, trying to imagine his story; at times, I was half planning to write it. Now, I no longer need to, because I have assimilated his story to mine; he fits into my pattern.

There is the question of loneliness. But again, this is not how you imagined it (if you had ever tried to imagine it). There are two essential kinds of loneliness: that of not having found someone to love, and that of having been deprived of the one you did love. The first kind is worse. Nothing can compare to the loneliness of the soul in adolescence. I remember my first visit to Paris in 1964; I was eighteen. Each day I did my cultural duty – galleries, museums, churches; I even bought the cheapest seat available at the Opéra Comique (and remember the impossible heat up there, the impossible sightlines, and the impossible-to-comprehend opera). I was lonely in the Métro, on the streets, and in the public parks where I would sit on a bench by myself reading a Sartre novel, which was probably about existential isolation. I was lonely even among those who befriended me. Remembering those weeks now, I realise that I never went upwards – the Eiffel Tower seemed an absurd, and absurdly popular, structure – but I did go down. I went down exactly as Nadar and his camera had done a hundred years previously. I too visited the Paris sewers, entering from somewhere near the Pont de l'Alma for a guided boat tour; and from the Place Denfert-Rochereau I descended into the Catacombs, my candle lighting up the neat banks of femurs and solid cubes of skulls.

There is a German word, *Sehnsucht*, which has no English equivalent; it means 'the longing for something'. It has Romantic and mystical connotations; C. S. Lewis defined it as the 'inconsolable longing' in the human heart for 'we know not what'. It seems rather German to be able to specify the unspecifiable. The longing for something – or, in our case, for someone. *Sehnsucht* describes the first kind of loneliness. But the second kind comes from the opposite condition: the absence of a very specific someone. Not so much loneliness as her-lessness. It is this specificity which incites consoling plans with the warm bath and the Japanese carving knife. And though I am now equipped with a firm argument against suicide, the temptation remains: if I cannot hack it without her, I will hack at myself instead. But now, at least, I am more aware of wise voices to call on. 'The cure for loneliness is solitude,' Marianne Moore advises. While Peter Grimes (if not in all respects a role model) sings: 'I live alone. The habit grows.' There is a balance to such words, a comforting harmony.

'It hurts exactly as much as it is worth, so in a way one relishes the pain, I think.' The second part of that sentence was what I stubbed my foot against: it struck me as unnecessarily masochistic. Now I know that it contains truth. And if the pain is not exactly relished, it no longer seems futile. Pain shows that you have not forgotten; pain enhances the flavour of memory; pain is a proof of love. 'If it didn't matter, it wouldn't matter.'

But there are many traps and dangers in grief, and time does not diminish them. Self-pity, isolationism, world-scorn, an egotistical exceptionalism: all aspects of vanity. Look how much I suffer, how much others fail to understand: does this not prove how much I loved? Maybe, maybe not. I have seen people 'doing grief' at funerals, and there is no emptier sight. Mourning can also become competitive: look how much I loved her/him and with these my tears I prove it (and win the trophy). There is the temptation to feel, if not to say: I fell from a greater height than you – examine my ruptured organs. The griefstruck demand sympathy, yet, irked by any challenge to their primacy, underestimate the pain others are suffering over the same loss.

Nearly thirty years ago, in a novel, I tried to imagine what it would be like for a man in his sixties to be widowed. I wrote:

> When she dies, you are not at first surprised. Part of love is preparing for death. You feel confirmed in your love when she dies. You got it right. This is part of it all.
>
> Afterwards comes the madness. And then the loneliness: not the spectacular solitude you had anticipated, not the interesting martyrdom of widowhood, but just loneliness. You expect something almost geological – vertigo in a shelving canyon – but it's not like that; it's just misery as regular as a job . . . [People say] you'll come out of it . . . And you do come out of it, that's true. But you don't come out of it like a train

coming out of a tunnel, bursting through the Downs into sunshine and that swift, rattling descent to the Channel; you come out of it as a gull comes out of an oil slick; you are tarred and feathered for life.

I read this passage at her funeral, October snow on the ground, my left hand touching her coffin, my right hand holding open the book (which was dedicated to her). My fictional widower had a different life — and love — from mine, and quite a different widowing. But I had to suppress just a few words in one sentence, and was surprised at what I took to be my accuracy. Only later did novelist's self-doubt set in: perhaps, rather than inventing the correct grief for my fictional character, I had merely been predicting my own probable feelings — an easier job.

For three years and more I continued to dream about her in the same way, according to the same narrative. Then I had a kind of meta-dream, one which seemed to propose an end to this line of night-work. And, as with all good endings, I didn't see it coming. In my dream we were together, doing things together, in some open space, being happy — all in the way I had become accustomed to — when suddenly *she* realised that this could not be true, and it all must be a dream, because *she* now knew that she was dead.

Should I be pleased with this dream? For here is the final tormenting, unanswerable question: what is 'success' in mourning? Does it lie in remembering or in forgetting? A staying still or a moving on? Or some combination of both? The ability to hold the lost love powerfully in mind, remembering without distorting? The ability to continue living as she would have wanted you to (though this is a tricky area, where the sorrowful can easily give themselves a free pass)? And afterwards? What happens to the heart – what does it need, and seek? Some form of self-sufficiency which avoids neutrality and indifference? Followed by some new relationship which will draw strength from the memory of the one who has been lost? This is like asking for the best of both worlds – though since you have just endured the worst of a single world, you might feel yourself entitled to it. But entitlement – the belief in some cosmic (or even animal) reward system – is another delusion, another vanity. Why should there be a pattern, here of all places?

There are moments which appear to indicate some kind of progress. When the tears – the daily, unavoidable tears – stop. When concentration returns, and a book can be read as before. When foyer-terror departs. When possessions can be disposed of (Orfeo, had things worked out differently, would have given that red frock to charity). And beyond this? What are you waiting for, looking for? The time when life turns back from opera into realist fiction. When that bridge you still drive under regularly becomes just another bridge again. When you retrospectively annul the results of that examination which some friends passed and others failed. When the temptation of suicide finally disappears — if it ever does. When cheerfulness and pleasure return, even while you recognise that cheerfulness has become more fragile, and present pleasure no match for past joy. When grief becomes 'just' the memory of grief — if it ever does. When the world reverts to being 'just' the world, and life feels once more as if it is taking place on the flat, on the level.

These may sound like clear markers, boxes awaiting a tick. But among any success there is much failure, much recidivism. Sometimes, you want to go on loving the pain. And then, beyond this, yet another question sharply outlines itself on the cloud: is 'success' at grief, at mourning, at sorrow, an achievement, or merely a new given condition? Because the notion of free will seems irrelevant here; the attribution of purpose and virtue — the idea of grief-work rewarded — feels misplaced. Perhaps, this time, the analogy with illness holds. Studies of cancer patients show that attitudes of mind have very little effect on clinical outcome. We may say we are fighting cancer, but cancer is merely fighting us; we may think we have beaten it, when it has only gone away to regroup. It is all just the universe doing its stuff, and we are the stuff it is being done to. And so, perhaps, with grief. We imagine we have battled against it, been purposeful, overcome sorrow, scrubbed the rust from our soul, when all that has happened is that grief has moved elsewhere, shifted its interest. We did not make the clouds come in the first place, and have no power to disperse them. All that has happened is that from somewhere – or nowhere – an unexpected breeze has sprung up, and we are in movement again. But where are we being taken? To Essex? The German Ocean? Or, if that wind is a northerly, then, perhaps, with luck, to France.

J.B.
London, 20 October 2012